Current
CONTROVERSIES

The Border Wall
with Mexico

Other Books in the Current Controversies Series

Current
CONTROVERSIES

The Border Wall with Mexico

Martin Gitlin, Book Editor

GREENHAVEN
PUBLISHING

Published in 2018 by Greenhaven Publishing, LLC
353 3rd Avenue, Suite 255, New York, NY 10010

First Edition

Articles in Greenhaven Publishing anthologies are often edited for length to meet page
requirements. In addition, original titles of these works are changed to clearly present
the main thesis and to explicitly indicate the author's opinion. Every effort is made to
ensure that Greenhaven Publishing accurately reflects the original intent of the authors.
Every effort has been made to trace the owners of the copyrighted material.

Cover image: Gila Photography/Shutterstock.com

Library of Congress Cataloging-in-Publication Data

Names: Gitlin, Martin, editor.
Title: The border wall with Mexico / edited by Martin Gitlin.
Description: New York : Greenhaven Publishing, 2018. | Series: Current controversies
| Includes bibliographical references and index. | Audience: Grades 9-
12.
Identifiers: LCCN ISBN 9781534500853 (library bound) | ISBN 9781534500907
(pbk.)
Subjects: LCSH: Mexican-American Border Region--History. | North America--
 Mexican-American Border Region. | Mexican-American Border Region--Emigration
 and immigration.
Classification: LCC F787.B67 2018 | DDC 972'.1--dc23

Manufactured in the United States of America

Website: http://greenhavenpublishing.com

Contents

Chapter 1: Does Building a Wall to Keep People Out Contradict American Values?

Joe Wolverton

The very right to freedom of movement, not just in immigration but emigration, should be questioned when politicians discuss fencing and border walls between the United States and other countries. A border wall would work against the very liberty and freedom America represents.

Yes: Building a Wall to Keep People Out Contradicts American Values

Enrique Morones

Building a wall would also build hatred among groups of people in a nation that values inclusion and diversity. Singling out Muslims or Mexicans creates divides that does not befit the American ideal.

John Dean

Donald Trump thought more with his emotions than his logic when he proposed building a border wall on the southwest border of the United States. Xenophobia and racism were behind his motivation for constructing the wall, which polls have shown that most Americans are against.

Jeffery Doherty and Boris Kaplan

Statistical data proves that illegal immigration has resulted in minimal criminal activity, leaving one to believe that the call to build a wall is based more on racism than more practical concerns.

United States, including the addition of detention centers and border agents, and the immediate construction of a border wall.

Yes: The United States Has the Resources to Build a Wall

Reece Jones

Reasons aside from protecting citizens from criminal activity enter into the correct decision to build a border wall, including establishing sovereignty over other countries and protecting the United States from those with value systems that do not match American ideals.

David North

The major problem is not illegal immigration from Mexico; it is that country's immigration problem from Central America. Paying Mexico to construct a fence that would cut off the northward migration of Central Americans would be a far more beneficial tact for the United States.

No: The United States Does Not Have the Resources to Build a Wall

Ali F. Rhuzkan

The overwhelming logistical challenges of building a wall that extends along the border of Mexico and serves to keep all illegal immigrants out of the US is far too immense to prove practical.

Shonil Bhagwat

In all of the debates about Donald Trump's great wall, few address the environmental impact such a structure would have on its surroundings. A thousand-mile barricade will have severe ecological consequences.

Chapter 3: Are There More Effective Ways to Prevent Illegal Immigration?

Statistics prove that the border wall proposed by Donald Trump can be done. The issue of whether or not it *should* be done based on potential effectiveness and cost can be debated from many different angles.

Chapter 4: Who Would Pay for the Wall?

anyway, to try to make their way back to the United States. That would stupidly create a problem by addressing one that is declining.

Foreword

"Controversy" is a word that has an undeniably unpleasant connotation. It carries a definite negative charge. Controversy can spoil family gatherings, spread a chill around classroom and campus discussion, inflame public discourse, open raw civic wounds, and lead to the ouster of public officials. We often feel that controversy is almost akin to bad manners, a rude and shocking eruption of that which must not be spoken or thought of in polite, tightly guarded society. To avoid controversy, to quell controversy, is often seen as a public good, a victory for etiquette, perhaps even a moral or ethical imperative.

Yet the studious, deliberate avoidance of controversy is also a whitewashing, a denial, a death threat to democracy. It is a false sterilizing and sanitizing and superficial ordering of the messy, ragged, chaotic, at times ugly processes by which a healthy democracy identifies and confronts challenges, engages in passionate debate about appropriate approaches and solutions, and arrives at something like a consensus and a broadly accepted and supported way forward. Controversy is the megaphone, the speaker's corner, the public square through which the citizenry finds and uses its voice. Controversy is the life's blood of our democracy and absolutely essential to the vibrant health of our society.

Our present age is certainly no stranger to controversy. We are consumed by fierce debates about technology, privacy, political correctness, poverty, violence, crime and policing, guns, immigration, civil and human rights, terrorism, militarism, environmental protection, and gender and racial equality. Loudly competing voices are raised every day, shouting opposing opinions, putting forth competing agendas, and summoning starkly different visions of a utopian or dystopian future. Often these voices attempt to shout the others down; there is precious little listening and considering among the cacophonous din. Yet listening and considering, too, are essential to the health of a democracy. If controversy is democracy's lusty lifeblood, respectful listening and careful thought are its higher faculties, its brain, its conscience.

Current Controversies does not shy away from or attempt to hush the loudly competing voices. It seeks to provide readers with as wide and representative as possible a range of articulate voices on any given controversy of the day, separates each one out to allow it to be heard clearly and fairly, and encourages careful listening to each of these well-crafted, thoughtfully expressed opinions, supplied by some of today's leading academics, thinkers, analysts, politicians, policy makers, economists, activists, change agents, and advocates. Only after listening to a wide range of opinions on an issue, evaluating the strengths and weaknesses of each argument, assessing how well the facts and available evidence mesh with the stated opinions and conclusions, and thoughtfully and critically examining one's own beliefs and conscience can the reader begin to arrive at his or her own conclusions and articulate his or her own stance on the spotlighted controversy.

This process is facilitated and supported in each Current Controversies volume by an introduction and chapter overviews that provide readers with the essential context they need to begin engaging with the spotlighted controversies, with the debates surrounding them, and with their own perhaps shifting or nascent opinions on them. Chapters are organized around several key questions that are answered with diverse opinions representing all points on the political spectrum. In its content, organization, and methodology, readers are encouraged to determine the authors' point of view and purpose, interrogate and analyze the various arguments and their rhetoric and structure, evaluate the arguments' strengths and weaknesses, test their claims against available facts and evidence, judge the validity of the reasoning, and bring into clearer, sharper focus the reader's own beliefs and conclusions and how they may differ from or align with those in the collection or those of classmates.

Research has shown that reading comprehension skills improve dramatically when students are provided with compelling, intriguing, and relevant "discussable" texts. The subject matter of these collections could not be more compelling, intriguing, or urgently relevant to today's students and the world they are poised to inherit. The anthologized articles also provide the basis for stimulating, lively, and passionate classroom debates. Students who are compelled to anticipate objections to their own argument and identify the flaws in those of an opponent read more carefully, think more critically, and steep themselves in relevant context, facts, and information more thoroughly. In short, using discussable text of the kind provided by every single volume in the Current Controversies series encourages close reading, facilitates reading comprehension, fosters research, strengthens critical thinking, and greatly enlivens and energizes classroom discussion and participation. The entire learning process is deepened, extended, and strengthened.

If we are to foster a knowledgeable, responsible, active, and engaged citizenry, we must provide readers with the intellectual, interpretive, and critical-thinking tools and experience necessary to make sense of the world around them and of the all-important debates and arguments that inform it. We must encourage them not to run away from or attempt to quell controversy but to embrace it in a responsible, conscientious, and thoughtful way, to sharpen and strengthen their own informed opinions by listening to and critically analyzing those of others. This series encourages respectful engagement with and analysis of current controversies and competing opinions and fosters a resulting increase in the strength and rigor of one's own opinions and stances. As such, it helps readers assume their rightful place in the public square and provides them with the skills necessary to uphold their awesome responsibility—guaranteeing the continued and future health of a vital, vibrant, and free democracy.

Introduction

The most recognized expression often blurted out about thorny issues is "there are two sides to every story." In many instances, that convenient claim does not do justice to the complex nature of a controversy.

Such is the case of the proposed wall between Mexico and the United States. It can be legitimately claimed that there are two sides to every aspect of that argument. But one can identify at least four separate and distinct points of discussion within the overall scope of the topic. That makes the debate far more complicated.

Few Americans focused their attention on the possibility of erecting a permanent barrier to prevent illegal immigrants from entering the United States until presidential candidate and eventual election winner Donald Trump unveiled his plan to do just that in an attempt to gain support from those that perceived the problem as a threat to their jobs and safety. The border wall was suddenly thrust into the spotlight as perhaps the most contentious issue of the campaign and beyond.

Further muddling matters was that Trump claimed he was not only going to all but duplicate the Great Wall of China to keep illegal immigrants out, but would in conjunction with his plan round up those already in the United States and send them back to Mexico. Though he later softened his stance, the emotional reaction to that idea, as well as the proposed wall, heightened the intensity of the debate. A figurative wall had been placed between Americans on both sides of an issue involving a literal wall.

Americans argued about the morality of keeping out people who simply yearned to take advantage of the same opportunities millions of other immigrants had over the centuries out of the country while maintaining relationships with family back home. One side claimed such a wall would weaken a country that has been a beacon of freedom for centuries, one that has welcomed immigrants sailing by the Statue of Liberty. The other side offered that those that poured in from Europe and Asia and Africa over the years were doing so legally. They opined that nobody was preventing legal immigration from Mexico.

They argued about how such a monumental project would be funded—the notion put forth by Trump that Mexico would pay for it was scoffed at in both countries. One side stated that convincing or forcing our neighbor to spend billions of dollars on a wall that provided them no benefit was unrealistic and that it would not be cost-efficient for the United States either. The other side claimed that it would be worth every penny, even if Mexico indeed refused to open its wallet.

They argued about the practical and logistical problems. Could such a massive wall running more than a thousand miles be constructed and possibly stop all those who sought to enter the United States from indeed doing so? One side insisted that such an effort would take manpower away from infrastructure projects that could prove far more beneficial to America and create more jobs. The other side contended quite the opposite—that the building of a wall would indeed mean work to many. They also cited a perceived economic benefit to those living in the country legally by keeping competition for jobs out.

Trump did not merely stir up the financial worries of his supporters. He fed their basest fears by claiming that many of those that had violated the borders of the southwest were gang members, murderers, and rapists. Some of those who embraced the idea of building a wall bought into racist views. It was argued by opponents of the plan that had the illegal immigrants been white people from Europe, for instance, there would not have been strong objections. The chants of "build the wall, build the wall, build the wall" at Trump rallies certainly smacked of racism, though some backers of Trump offered that their support was based on the most practical and unemotional of reasons.

Many of those who oppose the wall do believe that America does have a problem with illegal immigration but that the answers lie with a path to citizenship rather than the creation of such a structure and sending out a deportation force to round up and return Mexicans to their native country.

This book examines both sides of all aspects of a controversy that gained tremendous attention during Trump's surge to the presidency. The complex issue must be debated thoroughly and with open minds if a solution is to be created that is best for all involved.

CHAPTER 1

Does Building a Wall to Keep People Out Contradict American Values?

Overview: A Border Wall Affects the Freedom and Liberty of All Americans

Joe Wolverton

Joe Wolverton has served as a featured contributor to The New American *magazine since 2004. His articles focusing on the National Defense Authorization Act, the United States Constitution, and related topics have appeared in national and international publications.*

In last night's CNN/Tea Party Patriots Debate among the GOP presidential candidates, several of the hopefuls declared that the best way to stem the tide of illegal immigrants flooding over the southern border was to build a fence. Rick Santorum, Jon Hunstman, and Mitt Romney all advocated erecting a fence along the length of the border with Mexico. So ardent was Huntsman support for the idea that he accused Rick Perry of being "treasonous" for the latter's assertion that the southern border cannot be secured.

At an earlier debate hosted by the Ronald Reagan Presidential Library in California, Minnesota Congresswoman Michelle Bachmann said that, "To not build a border or a fence on every part of that border would be an effect to yield United States sovereignty."

As has been reported, Congressman Ron Paul was effectively shut out of last night's debate, particularly in two areas where he has been most vociferous and controversial: the Federal Reserve and immigration.

While his colleagues where trying to out secure each other, Ron Paul's position on the border and illegal immigration was not addressed. In an earlier appearance with the other potential Republican presidential nominees, Dr. Paul made very clear his unique (among those competing in the GOP field) opinion of the purpose of walling off the United States. Said Congressman Paul:

"Is Border Fence to Keep 'Us' In; Not 'Them' Out?" by Joe Wolverton, *The New American*, September 14, 2011. Reprinted by permission of The New American.com.

The people that want big fences and guns, sure, we could secure the border. A barbed wire fence with machine guns, that would do the trick. I don't believe that is what America is all about. Every time you think about this toughness on the border and ID cards and REAL IDs, think it's a penalty against the American people too. I think this fence business is designed and may well be used against us and keep us in. In economic turmoil, the people want to leave with their capital and there's capital controls and there's people controls. Every time you think about the fence, think about the fences being used against us, keeping us in.

Given the pre-packaged, predictable pronouncements heard in these televised stump speeches, there is little wonder that Dr. Paul's reasoned insistence and sincere warning that any fence erected around the border could (will) be used not only to manage the incomings, but the outgoings, as well.

There are those in power, insists Paul, that are as "interested in regulating our right to freely exit the country as they are in preventing illegal entry." To what end would the power elites wish to prevent the freedom of movement of the citizens of the United States?

Simply put, many of those elected by us to "preserve, protect, and defend the Constitution" have chosen to preserve, protect, and defend their own positions of power by passing legislation that empowers Congress and the executive branch to keep innocent citizens under constant surveillance and to proscribe the taking of capital outside the borders of the United States.

These petty tyrants rely on the continuing acquiescence of the American people (particularly the middle class) to a tax code that redistributes wealth and maintains the culture of dependence that guarantees the electoral devotion of a significant bloc of citizens to those who promise to perpetuate the current welfare policy that will keep the checks coming.

Dr. Paul, in his book, *50 Essential Issues That Effect Our Freedom,* explains that:

> The leaders of neither Republican nor the Democratic party can expect to protect our civil liberties when times get tough: Both support illegal wars; both support Patriot Act suppression of our privacy; both strongly endorse the multitrillion dollar bailout of Wall Street. Neither party will protect our right to vote with our feet and take our money with us. The right of a citizen to leave the country anytime with his wealth and without government interference is a sharp dividing line between a free society and a dictatorship.

These policies have harmed the American people and have tightened the manacles of oppression forged by the foes of freedom. To prevent any citizen from "voting with his feet" and leaving the country with his accumulated wealth is absolutely incompatible with the timeless principles of liberty as distilled in our founding charter. Furthermore, the erection of this "electronic financial curtain" was never contemplated by our Founding Fathers and it must be brought down.

As the time approaches for Americans to exercise their most precious of rights—the right to elect those who will represent us in the halls of Congress and in the White House—we must faithfully carry out our obligation to think deeply and critically about the issues that may soon decide the fate of our Republic. The time is very near when the actions taken on our behalf may perpetuate the issuing of kill orders for American citizens marked for assassination because of some vague charge of suspicious behavior.

As Dr. Paul rightly states, there is a very real danger in the attempt on the part of the government to curtail the movement of citizens, especially "in the age of secret prisons and a state position of assassinating American citizens if deemed a 'threat,' without charges ever being made...."

There are so many issues upon which these Republican office seekers agree. Sadly, one upon which so few of them agree is the unwavering commitment to follow the Constitution every time without compromise or exception. There are a variety of ways that the federal government could exercise its constitutional power to protect the states against invasion (see Article IV, Section 4 of the Constitution). Many of these methods would accomplish this legal end without restricting the free flow of citizens.

In the age when our Republic is in the grip of an economic maelstrom, the right of a person to vote with his feet and leave the nation with his money should be sacrosanct. To forbid such unshackled movement is the action of a government that fears such freedom.

Recently, the requirement that we carry a passport when traveling to and from Mexico and Canada by air demonstrates the intent of our leaders to monitor our movement. (When returning from either by land or sea, a passport card or "enhanced" drivers license—currently issued only by Michigan, New York, Vermont and Washington—is required.) There is additional evidence that our elected representatives and the regulatory leviathan they have empowered with legislative powers are devoted to watching every movement and assuring that those movements are not only noticed, but that they are tracked and tallied, as well.

Finally, despite the rhetoric, there is no clause in the Constitution granting to the general legislature exclusive authority over immigration policy. In fact, there is no mention of such a delegation at all. Admittedly, the Constitution does give power over naturalization to Congress (see Article I, Section 8), but the concepts of immigration and naturalization, while related, are distinct. Therefore, the power to control the passage of persons across the border (whether with Canada or with Mexico) is retained by the states per the Tenth Amendment.

Therefore, we must demand that those elected to the state legislatures and to the governors' mansions throughout the Republic adhere rigidly to the Constitution and find acceptable (constitutional) means of managing the entry of immigrants into the country without encroaching upon the right of Americans to exit at their own will and with their own wealth. Were our leaders to abide by the enumerated and limited powers set forth in the Constitution, then Americans would not want to leave and the majority of immigrants to our nation would be those earnestly seeking the blessings afforded only by a free and peaceful society.

Building a Wall at the Border Would Divide Us

Enrique Morones

Enrique Morones founded and directs the Border Angels in San Diego. He has been interviewed on The Today Show, The O'Reilly Factor, *and* Larry King Live *for his expertise on immigration.*

This election season, there's no televised presidential debate—Democratic or Republican—that doesn't eventually address immigration reform. At its best, the debate informs us about the lives and families torn apart by deportation. We see immigrants' humanity and dignity honored when leaders take into account the true gravity of these policies and the untold damage inflicted on hard working, taxpaying immigrant families. But when the debate is at its worst, candidates spew anti-immigrant vitriol.

We are seeing a direct correlation between anti-immigrant rhetoric and the rise in the harassment of and violence against immigrants. Last summer, two brothers beat a homeless Latino man, claiming they were inspired after hearing one candidate's comments on immigration. Last month a Muslim student in Wichita was allegedly beaten while his assailant chanted a candidate's name. Hate crimes like these strike fear and despair in the hearts of immigrants.

This hatred is being used to build support for anti-immigrant policies that would wreak havoc on our entire nation, not just new immigrants. The most damaging proposals include deporting nearly 11 million undocumented immigrants from our nation, building a wall along the entire U.S./Mexico border and singling out Muslim neighborhoods for invasive video camera surveillance.

Singling out Muslim neighborhoods for invasive video surveillance sends the fearful and false message that American

"Building a wall at the border would divide us," by Enrique Morones, News Communications, Inc, May 3, 2016. Reprinted by permission.

Muslims are less deserving of the rights and dignities enjoyed by other Americans. Our nation was founded, in part, on the principle of freedom of religion and here we have a radical proposal to profile and harass religious communities across the country. The proposal is eerily reminiscent of the Japanese internment camps, which remain a stain on our nation's history today.

Some are proposing to round up and deport the nearly 11 million undocumented immigrants currently living in the U.S. This proposal hearkens back to "Operation Wetback" in the 1950s when the U.S. raided and deported over 1,000,000 undocumented immigrants, most often to cities in central and southern Mexico where these workers had no family or friends. Mass deportation would involve armed law enforcement officials raiding homes and, in many cases, destroying families by ripping U.S. citizen children from their undocumented parents' arms. Logistically, this plan is nearly impossible to enforce. More importantly, the proposal would cruelly deny these children their parents or the benefits of their citizenship.

One of the most outrageous proposals calls for building a wall along the entire U.S./Mexico border and having Mexico pay for it. Their promise is that a wall would stop the flow of undocumented immigrants into the U.S. But that ignores the fact that nearly half of undocumented immigrants arrive in our nation with proper documentation and simply overstay their visas.

Of course, none of the rhetoric acknowledges the many positive contributions that immigrants make to our nation. In 2012, undocumented immigrants paid over $11 billion in state and local taxes. Granting them permanent legal status would increase that amount by $2.2 billion and raise their tax rate from 8 to 8.7 percent, aligning them with tax rates paid by similarly situated documented immigrants. Undocumented immigrants pay an estimated $7 billion into a social security system from which they will never benefit. Immigrants own 18 percent of our nation's small businesses and, despite being only 13 percent of the population, comprise 16 percent of the labor force. In short, many candidates are ignoring that we are a nation of immigrants and that we rely on immigrants to make our country work.

As this election continues and the rhetoric reaches a fever pitch, we must call on our candidates to propose effective and compassionate immigration reform. We must demand that they speak and act responsibly. We need real answers and plausible solutions to the very complex problems, not scads of unrealistic proposals that further muddy the debate and accomplish nothing.

Most importantly, we need to remember who we are and what we stand for. We are a nation built on the promise of opportunity and rights for all. We have a long tradition of relying on immigrants coming to the U.S. to raise their families while helping us build a stronger country.

Historically, walls, such as those in Berlin and China, have symbolized divisiveness and repression. The proposed wall along our southern border would only serve to deepen an ugly chasm, dividing neighbors who work and live together in the U.S. Some believe in building walls, but Border Angels believes in building doors.

We cannot let irrational fear and hate mongering rule our immigration policy. We must honor our best traditions and be guided by the values liberty, justice and human rights. Our nation is strongest when we work together with thoughtful minds and kind hearts to find solutions that will unite the United States.

Trump's Border Wall: It Should Never Happen

John Dean

John Dean famously served as counsel to Richard Nixon during his presidency from 1970 to 1974 before authoring books about Watergate and other related issues over the next several decades.

Donald Trump has promoted a xenophobic immigration policy from the outset of his presidential campaign. He declared that Mexico was exporting "criminals," "killers," "rapists," and "drug deals" to the United States. To deal with this situation, Trump announced he would build a wall along the Mexican-United States border, for which he would force Mexico to pay costs.

As with most Trump proposals to "make America great again," he has been long on promises and short on details. In the months since the official launch of his campaign on June 17, 2015, however, journalists have forced him into giving some details of the wall he envisions, and most recently the *Washington Post* pushed him to provide a general explanation of how he was going to get Mexico to pay for the wall.

Trump's wall typifies his governing ideas and tactics. He has simply tossed out a thought without carefully thinking it through. As a result, it is unrealistic and unworkable. It would likely cause more harm than good. No informed person with whom I have spoken believes any good could come from such a wall, although there is no shortage of bad things that could occur.

Nor is there public clamor for such a draconian sealing of our southern border. According to the latest Pew Research Poll only about a third of Americans support the idea of a wall, with Republicans predominately favoring it. Pew reports, "By nearly two-to-one (63% to 33%), Republicans and GOP leaners favor building a wall along the entire U.S.-Mexico border. By contrast, just 13% of Democrats favor building a border wall, while 84% are opposed."

This hair-brained idea should never come to fruition because even if it could be built, it would be a monument to isolationism and nativism Donald Trump espouses, and hardly be worth the expense for it is not a solution to our nation's immigration problems.

Trump's Mexican Border Wall

The border between the U.S. and Mexico runs through four American states: California, Arizona, New Mexico and Texas. The border is a highly diverse terrain from ocean waters (Pacific and the Gulf of Mexico) to urban areas (e.g., from San Diego and Tijuana to Brownsville and Matamoros) dominated by arid deserts. Yet two major rivers (Colorado and Rio Grande) cross the border from the U.S. to Mexico, which also have farm lands, deltas, and rugged mountain areas. The border runs 1,989 miles and every year no fewer than 350 million people cross it—legally! There are 35 border cities, with 45 crossing points and 330 ports of entry, not to mention that over 12 million people reside along the border.

Designing and building a "beautiful and massive" wall on this complex terrain would be a major engineering challenge, and Trump has been anything but consistent in describing the wall he envisions. For example, Trump says his wall will have "a big, beautiful door" so the "good ones" can come back in, but how will that door handle 350 million people who cross the border each year, many doing it daily? Trump has described his wall as low as 25 feet tall and at other times as high as 55 feet. Sometimes he has his wall running the entire border, other times only 1,000 miles, plus the 670 miles of high steel fencing Republicans spent $2.4 billion to keep illegal immigrants out of the U.S.

Clearly, Trump is promoting a concept, not an actual proposal. When you look closely at implementing his idea, difficult, if not impossible, problems abound. To build such a wall the Mexico-U.S. Boundary Treaty would have to be renegotiated. Even more difficult would be acquiring the necessary privately owned real estate (with widely-unpopular eminent domain proceedings requiring years of litigation). Much of the border runs though the public lands held by National Parks, yet with 84 percent of Democrats opposed to a wall, it is not likely Congress would approve this ecological, environmental and political disruption of prime American wilderness, the home to countless endangered and protected species. The seasonal ebbing and flowing Colorado and Rio Grande rivers will require a wall designed to allow the water out without letting people in.

Trump, of course, brushes aside all problems, and while he resists being pinned down with specifics, the *Washington Post* recently got him to explain how he would pay for this project. His explanation, however, further documents that this is Trump campaign blather for those gullible enough to buy into his fantasy policies.

The Cost of Trump's Wall

Trump's claim that he will force the Mexicans to pay for his wall raises two fundamental issues: How much will it cost? And how will he make the Mexicans pay for a wall for which they have said—at least a current and past president of Mexico—Mexico will not pay?

When Trump discussed the cost of his wall on MSNBC, in early February 2016, he said we only need 1,000 miles because of natural barriers, and that would cost $8 billion. He explained the wall would be made of precast cement, "probably 35 to 40 feet up in the air. That's high; that's a real wall. It will actually look good. It'll look, you know, as good as a wall is going to look." A few weeks later, Trump upped the cost to $10 to 12 billion. But none of these cost numbers could be verified by a *Washington Post* fact checker. The *Post* estimated the cost would be more like $25 billion.

The *Post* also quizzed Trump on his claim that Mexico would pay for his wall. Trump explained his funding scheme to *Post* reporters Bob Woodward and Robert Costa. Envisioning a 1,000 mile wall, Trump provided a two-page memo explaining that he was only looking for "a one-time payment of $5-10 billion" from Mexico, which Trump said Mexico would be happy to pay because if they did not, as president he would use his executive powers to cut of the flow of billions of dollars in payment immigrants send home to Mexico, a cut off that would decimate the Mexican economy. The *Post* reported that almost "$25 million was sent home by Mexicans," and Trump claims "the majority of that amount comes from illegal aliens."

Initially, Trump said would use the USA Patriot Act's antiterrorism provisions to prevent money transfers from the United States to Mexico, making poor Mexicans the equivalent of terrorists to block their remittances, which would hobble the Mexican economy. Like all Trump policies, when glitches arise, he amends his thinking. Trump recognizes that his interpretation of the USA Patriot Act might not pass judicial muster, so he has added a few other broad fee schemes to pay for the wall such as increasing fees on "all temporary visas issued to Mexican CEOs and diplomats," "increase fees on all border crossing cards—of which we issue about 1 million to Mexican nationals each year," "increase fees on all NAFTA worker visas from Mexico," "and increase fees at ports of entry to the United States from Mexico." In other words, it will be the Mexican people—not the government—who will pay for Trump's wall.

The Absurdity of It All

Of course, Trump's wall is connected to his plan to deport some 11 million illegal aliens in the United States. Once he rounds them up—another impossibly complex proposal he has never fully explained—he wants to keep out "the bad ones," thus the wall.

Border security is a real issue that Democrats have recognized as well. Hillary Clinton agrees we need to better secure our borders, but she views Trump's wall for what it is—all talk and no solution. Right-wing websites, like the Daily Caller, have posted charts showing the impact of walls built in Europe in halting immigration. But the porous borders of Europe are very different than ours, and fences no doubt do keep women and children out, but not the "bad ones," who Trump says are his target.

Brendan Lenihan, a former U.S. Border Patrol officer now attending law school, looks at the politicization of border security when he addresses related environmental issues along the Arizona-Mexico border. Lenihan says that every Border Patrol agent with whom he has spoken about border security understands there can never be total control of a border. Lenihan cites studies by the Cato Institute that looked at the Cold War border between East and West Germany, "the most heavily fortified in modern history," yet it "was successfully breached a thousand or so times each year." The Cato study found:

> There is simply no way for a large, open and democratic country like the United States to construct and maintain perfect border defenses. It is hard to think of another issue where the public debate is so utterly at odds with what the government can realistically achieve.

Building Trump's wall would be expensive folly. It will not keep out "the bad ones." But it will wreck the ecology of the southwestern United States. Such a wall would certainly serve as a monument to Trump's ugly-American thinking. So before any such project is started, President Trump should order the Park Service to cover the Statue of Liberty in black, for her symbolic welcoming to immigrants can be declared dead when he starts building a massive Trump wall.

What Trump's Plan Really Says: This is "The Great Wall of Racism"

Jeffery Doherty and Boris Kaplan

Jeffery Doherty and Boris Kaplan wrote the following piece for The New Dealer, the student news site of Franklin Delano Roosevelt High School in New York City.

Trump would build a wall along the US-Mexico border to stop illegal immigrants from illegally entering the United States if he were to be elected president. Currently that is a plausible reality since he is currently the Republican front runner. According to recent polls, he currently has 40% favor among Republican voters, while second place candidate Ted Cruz has about 20%. If the situation does not change soon, Donald Trump will be nominated as a candidate and possibly win the White House. If he does win and then tries to implement his plan of building the wall, how reasonable will it be?

Across the US-Mexican border there are numerous geographical challenges that face the construct of wall. From West to East there are: Deserts, Savannah (desert with some plants), mountains, hills, dunes, hard rocky soil and even craters. While there are already border "fortifications" as in checkpoints and stretches of fencing, a lot of this land is lightly patrolled with no walls at all. The wall would have to go, if by Trump's plan along the whole border, through rugged terrain and even cities. For example El Paso on the US side, and Ciudad Juarez on the Mexican side, are divided by a highway and small checkpoints. These two cities are essentially a "shared city," while although divided by a border, for nearly a century that border has experienced shared culture and had a sense of community towards each other. Though there were recent increases in border security due to crime in Juarez, it largely remains easy to move to and from both sides.

With rugged terrain and other obstacles, how much would it cost to build? Billions. $5.1–$5.9 billion according to CNBC and Poltico. That's without upkeep, which would cost roughly $750 million per year. The US Federal Budget is $3.8 trillion, which most of is not optional, and we have $21 trillion in debt! With crumbling infrastructure, homelessness, poverty, and many other issues facing the nation, is it really worth spending so much money on the wall? Trump says yes, and according to his website, "The cost of building a permanent border wall pales mightily in comparison to what American taxpayers spend every single year on dealing with the fallout of illegal immigration on their communities, schools and unemployment offices." Besides, he'll make Mexico pay for it! Though there are no legal means of forcing Mexico to pay, and through negotiations, Mexico will not be willing to pay billions to the US, a nation with a nearly 16 times larger economy. Trump will do it anyway, because he claims he is a good negotiator. Even though a spokesperson for the Mexican President Enrique Pena Neito said that the idea is ridiculous.

What are the reasons for building the wall in the first place? Trump and his supporters cite that illegal immigrants will do the following: take jobs, smuggle drugs, kidnap people, bring in cartels, rape, murder, and do other horrible things. According to Trump, this is most, not some, most of all illegal immigrants, as he said so to his supporters in numerous speeches. This is where the real reason for the wall emerges: racism, xenophobia and nativism.

Grouping together an entire race or ethnicity, and judging them negatively on the actions of a few, is both a generalization and racism. The fear of violence and crime is racist as most Mexicans and illegal immigrants are not criminals. Less than 7% commit violent crimes compared to US having 1% of its entire population in jail (though mostly for nonviolent drug offenses). Even with that, crime rates in the US are dropping. It's not that illegals don't commit crimes, a few do, but to judge all of them based on that is racist.

According to the Pew Research Center, there are around 10-12 million illegal immigrants living in America with about half of them from Mexico. Let's say by most of them being bad people, Trump means around 50% of Mexican; sounds reasonable. That's around 2 million murderers, rapists, kidnappers and other horrible human beings are in America right now! No wonder we need the wall, right? The problem comes from the fact that illegal immigrants make up 5.1% of the U.S. labor force. From the Pew Research Center, in 2012 alone, 8 million illegals either worked or were looking for work. That's the other part. Hard working people that make up 1/20th of a 160 million person workforce, doing unskilled or partially skilled labor, from janitorial services to construction. That's most illegals. Stopping, or attempting to stop this flow of workers would be a burden on the U.S. economy. These immigrants, though illegal, boost the U.S. population and fuel a growth in the number of young adults that would be available through naturalization for work in the near future. If the wall were to be built, immigration wouldn't suddenly stop, it would be slowed down, and illegal immigration would still happen. Besides, they can just build tunnels under the wall, already a common smuggling method used by illegals and drug cartels.

With an incredible cost to the country, the wall would become a symbol of how dumb our nation can get. A better way to "make America great again" as Donald Trump put it, would be to allow more immigrants in, and have citizenship be faster, while making citizenship more accessible. According to the poem by an immigrant called The New Colossus, "Give me your tired, your poor, Your huddled masses yearning to breathe free," shall we adhere to this or only do it to those immigrants who are already here, as the U.S. is a nation of immigrants. The boost in our workforce and the diversity that would come from immigrant cultures would be closer to the values of the U.S.A., while greatly improving our international reputation.

Obama-Appointed Judge: Border Fence Is Racist Against Mexicans

Judicial Watch

Judicial Watch is a conservatively slanted watchdog group that files Freedom of Information Act lawsuits in an effort to expose supposed misconduct by government officials. Among its targets have been presidents Bill Clinton, George W. Bush, and Barack Obama.

A Homeland Security initiative to put fencing along the U.S.-Mexico border could discriminate against minorities, according to an Obama-appointed federal judge who's ruled that the congressionally-approved project may have a "disparate impact on lower-income minority communities."

This of course means that protecting the porous—and increasingly violent—southern border is politically incorrect. At least that's what the public college professor at the center of the case is working to prove and this month she got help from a sympathetic federal judge. Denise Gilman, a clinical professor at the taxpayer-funded University of Texas-Austin, is researching the "human rights impact" of erecting a barrier to protect the U.S. from terrorists, illegal immigrants, drug traffickers and other serious threats.

A 2006 federal law orders the construction of fencing or a wall along the most vulnerable portions of the nearly 2,000-mile southern border. This includes reinforced fencing along 700 miles of the southwest border with the Department of Homeland Security (DHS) determining the exact spots. Professor Gilman wants the identities of the landowners in the planned construction site to shed light on the impact the fencing will have on indigenous, minority and low-income communities. The feds refused to provide the information, asserting that it's private.

"Obama Judge: Mexican Border Fence May Have "Disparate Impact" on Minorities," Judicial Watch, March 20, 2014. Reprinted by permission.

The professor sued in federal court arguing that the public interest in how the fence will impact landowners outweighed any privacy concerns. The data will allow the public to analyze whether the government is treating property owners equally and fairly or whether the wall is being built in such a way that it disadvantages "minority property owners," according to the professor. It will also help the public understand the actual dimensions of the wall and decisions related to where it's placed.

Judge Beryl Howell, appointed to the U.S. District Court for the District of Columbia by President Obama in 2010, agreed that the public interest is significant. Her 37-page ruling also seems to indicate that she bought the discrimination argument. "Revealing the identities of landowners in the wall's planned construction site may shed light on the impact on indigenous communities, the disparate impact on lower-income minority communities, and the practices of private contractors," Howell wrote.

This is simply the latest controversy to strike the border fence project since Congress approved it to protect national security and curb an illegal immigration and drug-trafficking crisis. In the last few years the mayors of several Texas border towns have blocked federal access to areas where the fence is scheduled to be built, an Indian tribe tried to block the barrier in the Arizona desert by claiming the feds were intruding on tribal land and a group of government scientists claimed the fencing would threaten the black bear population.

Last summer Mexican officials expressed public outrage over U.S. efforts to secure the southern border, calling it a human rights violation and an "unfriendly act." The fact is, a number of government reports have confirmed that it's not just Mexicans crossing into the U.S. seeking a better life. In 2010 DHS warned Texas law enforcement agencies that a renowned Al Qaeda terrorist was planning to sneak into the U.S. through Mexico. That same year a veteran federal agent accused the government of covering up the growing threat created by Middle Eastern terrorists entering the country through the vulnerable Mexican border.

Violent crime in the region has been well documented with heavily armed Mexican drug cartels taking over chunks of land that serve as routes to move cargo north. In fact, a few years ago a State Department report exposed a "dramatic increase in violence" along the Mexican border and warned of "violent attacks and persistent security concerns" in the area. The document also lists tens of thousands of narcotics-related murders attributed to sophisticated and heavily armed drug cartels competing with each other for trafficking routes into the U.S.

Border Fencing Is Critical to Ensure American Security

Duncan Hunter

Duncan Hunter is a staunchly conservative California congressman based in the San Diego area. He was elected for his first term in 2008. He has come out in favor of strengthening national security and enforcing borders.

Government bureaucracy has been an obstacle to building the fencing needed to secure our borders even though it has both the technology and manpower needed. The Department of Homeland Security has indicated its intention to build 370 miles of border fencing even though the Secure Fence Act calls for more than double that length. Border fencing is vital to our efforts to address problems commonly associated with illegal immigration. Making a decision not to build fencing as dictated by law will be interpreted to mean that we are not serious about securing our borders and enforcing our nation's immigration laws. If we want to be safe, our borders need to be secure. The time has come for us to act, to do what is right and build the border fence.

It's much tougher than it should be to secure America's borders. While the technology and manpower are all within reach, what seems beyond our grasp is the ability to act. Take [2006] legislation calling for construction of 854 miles of fence on our Southern border.

It's all too obvious that America is under threat because its land borders are largely porous and unprotected. In response [in 2006], Congress passed, and the President signed into law, legislation calling for the construction of those 854 miles of border fencing along the U.S.-Mexico border. Despite this legislative mandate by the U.S. Congress, the Department of Homeland Security [DHS] recently announced its intention to build only 370 miles of fencing along the border, not the 854 miles required by the legislation.

"Border Fencing Is Crucial to Ensure American Security," by Duncan Hunter, Gale, 2010.

This directive, despite its clarity, appears to have been interpreted as a suggestion. It is not: it's the law—and the border fence must be built.

Government Must Take Action

The Secure Fence Act requires that reinforced fencing and related infrastructure be installed along the most dangerous and problematic smuggling corridors along our Southern land border, which continues providing illegal immigrants, drug smugglers and potential terrorists access into the United States. As the original author of the measure's fencing provision, I expected there to be some opposition to implementing strategic fencing along our land border with Mexico. I did not, however, expect one of the biggest obstacles to be the federal agency primarily responsible for protecting the American homeland, especially when border fencing has proven to be an effective enforcement tool with verifiable results.

In San Diego County[, California], for example, border fencing remains a critical part of our continuing effort to address the problems commonly associated with illegal immigration. Since construction of the San Diego Border Fence began in 1996, the smuggling of people and narcotics has dropped drastically, crime rates have been reduced by half, according to FBI statistics, vehicle drug drive-throughs have been eliminated and apprehensions have decreased as the result of fewer crossing attempts.

Border fencing has proven to be an effective enforcement tool with verifiable results.

The Clinton Administration opposed the construction of the San Diego Border Fence as a method of closing the prolific smuggling corridor that once existed between San Diego and Tijuana, Mexico. The Clinton Administration, however, also recognized its responsibility under the law. Construction of the San Diego Border Fence began and conditions on both sides of the border immediately improved.

The Bush Administration says it remains committed to securing the border. I intend to hold them to their word. Just as I did with the Clinton Administration, I will continue reminding the Bush Administration of their obligation under the law to build the border fence. I believe they can, and will, do better.

Bureaucracy is rarely ever capable of producing immediate results. But when it threatens the safety and security of our communities, it becomes intolerable. The decision not to build fencing as dictated by law can only serve to demonstrate that we are not serious about securing our borders and enforcing our nation's immigration laws.

To date, only 12 miles of the 854 miles of border fencing called for in the Secure Fence Act have been constructed.

Border Fencing Is Necessary

Why is reinforced border infrastructure necessary? In 2005, 155,000 foreign nationals from countries other than Mexico were apprehended attempting to cross our land border with Mexico. Alarmingly, many of these individuals originated from countries of national security concern, including Syria, Iran, Lebanon and Yemen, and likely represent only a fraction of those who successfully entered our country without the knowledge of border security officials or the consent of our government.

It has also been reported that several of the individuals who were discovered to be plotting the next major terrorist attack against the United States, targeting soldiers at Fort Dix, crossed the U.S.-Mexico border through Brownsville, Texas. Whether they entered as children or adults, the fact that they originated from countries far from our shores demonstrates that across the world, it is understood that the best way to illegally enter the United States is through our land border with Mexico.

To date, only 12 miles of the 854 miles of border fencing called for in the Secure Fence Act have been constructed. While it's a start, the 370 miles of fencing promised by DHS represents a significant departure from what's required by federal law. Let's be perfectly clear: it's not enough. Even the 854 miles of fence legislated last year [in 2006] is only a beginning. Legislation presently under consideration by the U.S. Senate to reform our immigration system also reaffirms DHS' decision to only build 370 miles of fencing. This legislation is weak on enforcement, comprehensively fails to make border security a priority and wrongly retreats from the mandates of the Secure Fence Act.

We know from our experiences in San Diego that border fencing works and when extended across Arizona, New Mexico and Texas, it will have the same salutary effect. DHS has more than $1 billion cash on hand for border fence construction and more will surely be delivered. It's time we get serious about border control, do what's right, and build the border fence. Secure borders make America safer. What's so hard to understand about that?

Border Walls Would Humanely Enforce a Just Law

Terence P. Jeffrey

Terence P. Jeffrey has served as editor-in-chief of CNSNews and editor of Human Events. *He also worked as the national campaign manager for presidential candidate Pat Buchanan in the mid-1990s.*

The federal government has a duty to enforce this nation's borders and do it in a humane manner that minimizes harm to human life both inside U.S. territory and on the approaches to it.

The best way to do that at the border with Mexico is to build effectively impermeable barriers that send a simple, straightforward message: You can only cross this border legally.

For years, our government has sent a different message: You may be able to cross illegally.

More recently, that inapt message has been compounded by another: If you make it here illegally, we may let you stay.

Between 2005 and 2010, according to the Congressional Research Service, the Department of Homeland Security used a measure called "operational control" to describe the stretches of border it had secured.

"Operational control describes the number of border miles where the Border Patrol can detect, identify, respond to, and interdict cross-border unauthorized activity," CRS said in a report published last month. "In February 2010, the Border Patrol reported that 1,107 miles (57 percent) of the Southwest border were under operational control."

That means our government, according to the Border Patrol, did not have operational control of 43 percent—or approximately 826 miles—of our southern border.

By failing to secure the border, the federal government not only allows foreign nationals to come here illegally to live and work, but also provides an avenue for deadly drugs, for the criminals who bring them and for potential terrorists.

The failure to secure our southern border harms American workers whose jobs are put at risk and whose wages are suppressed by competition with immigrant workers here illegally.

It also harms Americans who become addicted to deadly drugs smuggled across the border, and it harms American communities where those drugs are distributed.

"Mexican transnational criminal organizations (TCOs) remain the greatest criminal drug threat to the United States; no other group can challenge them in the near term," the U.S. Drug Enforcement Administration said in its 2015 National Drug Threat Assessment Summary.

"These Mexican poly-drug organizations traffic heroin, methamphetamine, cocaine, and marijuana throughout the United States, using established transportation routes and distribution networks," said the DEA assessment. "They control drug trafficking across the Southwest Border and are moving to expand their share of U.S. illicit drug markets, particularly heroin markets."

"National-level gangs and neighborhood gangs continue to form relationships with Mexican TCOs to increase profits for the gangs through drug distribution and transportation, for the enforcement of drug payments, and for protection of drug transportation corridors from use by rival gangs," said the assessment.

Failure to secure our border not only harms people in the United States, it also harms people in Mexico and would-be illegal border crossers. Mexicans are victimized by the drug cartels that exploit our unenforced border, and migrants seeking to cross our unsecured border to illegally live or work here put themselves at risk in remote regions and in the custody of human traffickers.

The message our federal government should send is: If you are coming here illegally, you will not be able to cross, so do not try.

Building physical barriers along the border that make it impossible for people to illegally pass either on foot or in vehicles—and deploying sufficient manpower to patrol those barriers—would send that message. Failing to build those barriers and sufficiently man them says: The people who run our federal government are still not serious about securing our border.

America is a generous nation when it comes to legal immigration.

Between 1980 and 2012, according to a 2014 report published by the Department of Homeland Security, the United States granted lawful permanent resident status to approximately 28,370,000 immigrants.

Those 28,370,000 legal permanent residents equaled more than three times the Census Bureau's July 2013 estimate for the population of New Jersey (8,911,502), more than twice the population of Illinois (12,890,552) and exceeded the populations of New York (19,695,680), Florida (19,600,311) and Texas (26,505,637).

America is also generous in granting refugee and asylum status to those who face a "well-founded fear of persecution" in their home countries. In 2013, this country granted refugee status to 69,909 individuals and asylum to 25,199.

We should not turn our back on those who seek refuge and asylum, especially Middle Eastern Christians who face genocide by Islamic State terrorists. Nor do we need to stop legal immigration.

But the border of the United States is a just law that the federal government has duty to enforce. Building walls that deter and stop illegal crossers is a humane way to do it.

Open Borders Does Immigrants More Harm Than Good

Michael Bargo Jr.

Michael Bargo Jr. is a self-employed writer and author. He has focused on issues regarding Hispanics in the United States, as well as politics in Chicago and the impact it has had on national policy in regard to illegal immigration.

Trump's proposal to build a big wall on the southern border of the U.S. has been called an exercise of xenophobia and racism.

Trump asserts that many of the illegal immigrants are criminals, and the U.S. should act to save the country from them. But what many refuse to recognize, what is never discussed, is how illegal immigration exploits the immigrants themselves.

The abuses suffered by illegal immigrants caused by the lack of an effective wall have not been humanely discussed. The plain truth is that illegal immigrants are forced to commit crimes in order to cross the border illegally.

The first time someone is caught crossing the U.S. border without going through legal immigration procedures they are guilty of a Federal misdemeanor. The second time they are caught their act is a Federal felony. Because of the cheerleading of illegal immigration done by Democrats and the media, Hispanics are now in Federal prisons in much greater proportion than their population number would suggest. While Hispanics make up only 13% of the U.S. population they are 40% of the Federal prison population.

The majority of those in Federal prison have committed Federal crimes that are a direct result of illegal immigration. These include drug smuggling and illegal entry. The Mexican drug cartel forces young men and women to carry drugs over the border in exchange for receiving assistance in their border crossing.

"How Trump's Border Wall Will Rescue Illegal Immigrants from Democrat Exploitation," by Michael Bargo, Jr., American Thinker, June 28, 2016. Reprinted by permission.

It is interesting to consider that the explanation of why blacks are in Federal prison is always that they are exploited by U.S. society and are victims of oppression. But no one states that illegal immigrants are oppressed, that their incarceration is a direct result of racism, even though one may argue that characterizing illegal immigrants as an uneducated, unskilled minority that comes to the U.S. to do low paid jobs no one else will is racist. But it is. Blacks were also brought to the U.S. to work plantations doing low paid work nobody else would do.

If Trump were to build a wall and completely stop illegal immigration, the effect would be that the arrest and incarceration of illegal immigrants for committing Federal crimes while crossing would stop. Americans can decide for themselves if this is a good or bad thing. Furthermore, according to the Pew Research Center's report "Between Two Worlds," Hispanics in the U.S. are now dropping out of high school at twice the rate of blacks. And this is going on throughout the nation. Critics of Trump's wall would need to explain how channeling another minority into a life of poverty is good policy.

Hispanic teenage girls are now becoming single mothers at a higher rate than black teenagers. Single motherhood is the major cause of poverty and crime. How Trump's wall can be criticized for stopping poverty and crime is also difficult to understand.

Those who criticize Trump for wanting to build a wall never discuss the exploitation of illegal immigrants by drug cartels, do not discuss the incarceration of Hispanics and their presence in Federal prisons, or the high dropout rate of Hispanic high school students. One can only wonder why these signs of oppression, which have been used for decades to prove that blacks are exploited by white society, are not used as proof that Mexicans are exploited.

The political fact is, Democrats established all the sanctuary cities. These acts are violations of the 1996 Immigration Act, so it is fair to argue that Democrats are responsible for the high dropout rate of Hispanics, the high single motherhood rate, and the high rate of Federal incarceration of Hispanics. But somehow if Donald Trump makes an effort to stop this he is called a racist.

Democrats are the only political party that benefits from illegal immigration. They segregated Hispanics into communities in big cities where they can serve the party by filling classrooms for the Democrat-supporting teacher unions, and vote for Democrats in elections.

The resistance to Trump's wall only proves that Democrats resort to name calling, ridicule, and intimidation whenever someone threatens their scheme to maintain political power. Hillary Clinton, who is currently the likely opponent of Donald Trump in the 2016 presidential election, is happy to benefit from Hispanic votes, and counts on them, along with black votes, to put her into the White House.

That Hillary can feel confident of the electoral support gained from minorities is a very sad commentary on the Democratic Party and the tactics it has used to stay in power. All the big city black ghettoes have been created by Democrats and have Democrats as representatives in Congress. Their plan to continue this scheme with Hispanics has, unfortunately, been very successful.

Voters can decide for themselves whose actions have the desirable results: Donald Trump, whose wall will reduce the exploitation of Hispanics, or Hillary Clinton, whose party will continue to build up the Hispanic population as their second impoverished voter minority.

Trump's wall will also stop the destruction of desert habitats in the Southwest. Right now these pristine desert preserves, which have never been developed, are being trampled on by illegal immigration perpetrated by Democrats, who claim credit to having started the environmental movement. This environmental issue is never discussed.

The greatest criticism of Trump's comments on the wall is that he labels all Mexicans as criminals. Trump does overstate the issue. But the facts that Hispanics are being segregated by liberals into barrios, single motherhood is on the rise, and Hispanics are being incarcerated in Federal prisons, is not an overstatement.

The one truth in this discussion is that seasonal, unskilled labor is needed by agriculture in many states. However, this need was legally addressed by the Bracero guest worker program, a program stopped by LBJ so the illegal immigration strategy could be pursued.

Anyone who is offended by Trump's strong, disrespectful language should also consider the strongly offensive words spoken by the Black Lives Matter movement, Reverend Wright, and the anti-Trump protesters who burn American flags and use abusive language.

Trump's wall will liberate Hispanics from exploitation, Democrats' words support the exploitation.

Given the history Democrats have in the U.S. of creating segregated minority communities and limiting their participation in the economy, a truly liberal, humanely-minded person may want to reconsider the value of Trump's wall, and reconsider who the party of racists is; the Democrats who exploit illegal immigrants or Donald Trump's Republicans, who freed the slaves and now want to control the abuse of Hispanics by the open border.

Trump's wall will save tens of thousands of innocent Hispanics from rape, murder, and Federal prison. Hillary could speak of a guest worker program but she won't do that. Her party doesn't want that. Her party wants voters and residents. It's another shameful chapter in the history of the exploitation of minorities by Democrats.

Does the United States Have the Resources to Build a Wall?

Overview: Executive Order: Border Security and Immigration Enforcement Improvements

Donald J. Trump

Donald J. Trump is the forty-fifth president of the United States of America.

By the authority vested in me as President by the Constitution and the laws of the United States of America, including the Immigration and Nationality Act (8 U.S.C. 1101 et seq.) (INA), the Secure Fence Act of 2006 (Public Law 109-367) (Secure Fence Act), and the Illegal Immigration Reform and Immigrant Responsibility Act of 1996 (Public Law 104-208 Div. C) (IIRIRA), and in order to ensure the safety and territorial integrity of the United States as well as to ensure that the Nation's immigration laws are faithfully executed, I hereby order as follows:

Section 1. Purpose. Border security is critically important to the national security of the United States. Aliens who illegally enter the United States without inspection or admission present a significant threat to national security and public safety. Such aliens have not been identified or inspected by Federal immigration officers to determine their admissibility to the United States. The recent surge of illegal immigration at the southern border with Mexico has placed a significant strain on Federal resources and overwhelmed agencies charged with border security and immigration enforcement, as well as the local communities into which many of the aliens are placed.

Transnational criminal organizations operate sophisticated drug- and human-trafficking networks and smuggling operations on both sides of the southern border, contributing to a significant increase in violent crime and United States deaths from dangerous drugs. Among those who illegally enter are those who seek to harm

"Trump's Executive Order Border Security and Immigration Enforcement Improvements," The White House, January 25, 2017.

Americans through acts of terror or criminal conduct. Continued illegal immigration presents a clear and present danger to the interests of the United States.

Federal immigration law both imposes the responsibility and provides the means for the Federal Government, in cooperation with border States, to secure the Nation's southern border. Although Federal immigration law provides a robust framework for Federal-State partnership in enforcing our immigration laws—and the Congress has authorized and provided appropriations to secure our borders—the Federal Government has failed to discharge this basic sovereign responsibility. The purpose of this order is to direct executive departments and agencies (agencies) to deploy all lawful means to secure the Nation's southern border, to prevent further illegal immigration into the United States, and to repatriate illegal aliens swiftly, consistently, and humanely.

Sec. 2. Policy. It is the policy of the executive branch to:

(a) secure the southern border of the United States through the immediate construction of a physical wall on the southern border, monitored and supported by adequate personnel so as to prevent illegal immigration, drug and human trafficking, and acts of terrorism;

(b) detain individuals apprehended on suspicion of violating Federal or State law, including Federal immigration law, pending further proceedings regarding those violations;

(c) expedite determinations of apprehended individuals' claims of eligibility to remain in the United States;

(d) remove promptly those individuals whose legal claims to remain in the United States have been lawfully rejected, after any appropriate civil or criminal sanctions have been imposed;

(e) cooperate fully with States and local law enforcement in enacting Federal-State partnerships to enforce Federal immigration priorities, as well as State monitoring and detention programs that are consistent with Federal law and do not undermine Federal immigration priorities.

Sec. 3. Definitions.

(a) "Asylum officer" has the meaning given the term in section 235(b)(1)(E) of the INA (8 U.S.C. 1225(b)(1)).

(b) "Southern border" shall mean the contiguous land border between the United States and Mexico, including all points of entry.

(c) "Border States" shall mean the States of the United States immediately adjacent to the contiguous land border between the United States and Mexico.

(d) Except as otherwise noted, "the Secretary" shall refer to the Secretary of Homeland Security.

(e) "Wall" shall mean a contiguous, physical wall or other similarly secure, contiguous, and impassable physical barrier.

(f) "Executive department" shall have the meaning given in section 101 of title 5, United States Code.

(g) "Regulations" shall mean any and all Federal rules, regulations, and directives lawfully promulgated by agencies.

(h) "Operational control" shall mean the prevention of all unlawful entries into the United States, including entries by terrorists, other unlawful aliens, instruments of terrorism, narcotics, and other contraband.

Sec. 4. Physical Security of the Southern Border of the United States. The Secretary shall immediately take the following steps to obtain complete operational control, as determined by the Secretary, of the southern border:

(a) In accordance with existing law, including the Secure Fence Act and IIRIRA, take all appropriate steps to immediately plan, design, and construct a physical wall along the southern border, using appropriate materials and technology to most effectively achieve complete operational control of the southern border;

(b) Identify and, to the extent permitted by law, allocate all sources of Federal funds for the planning, designing, and constructing of a physical wall along the southern border;

(c) Project and develop long-term funding requirements for the wall, including preparing Congressional budget requests for the current and upcoming fiscal years; and

(d) Produce a comprehensive study of the security of the southern border, to be completed within 180 days of this order, that shall include the current state of southern border security, all geophysical and topographical aspects of the southern border, the availability of Federal and State resources necessary to achieve complete operational control of the southern border, and a strategy to obtain and maintain complete operational control of the southern border.

Sec. 5. Detention Facilities.

(a) The Secretary shall take all appropriate action and allocate all legally available resources to immediately construct, operate, control, or establish contracts to construct, operate, or control facilities to detain aliens at or near the land border with Mexico.

(b) The Secretary shall take all appropriate action and allocate all legally available resources to immediately assign asylum officers to immigration detention facilities for the purpose of accepting asylum referrals and conducting credible fear determinations pursuant to section 235(b)(1) of the INA (8 U.S.C. 1225(b)(1)) and applicable regulations and reasonable fear determinations pursuant to applicable regulations.

(c) The Attorney General shall take all appropriate action and allocate all legally available resources to immediately assign immigration judges to immigration detention facilities operated or controlled by the Secretary, or operated or controlled pursuant to contract by the Secretary, for the purpose of conducting proceedings authorized under title 8, chapter 12, subchapter II, United States Code.

Sec. 6. Detention for Illegal Entry. The Secretary shall immediately take all appropriate actions to ensure the detention of aliens apprehended for violations of immigration law pending the outcome of their removal proceedings or their removal from the country to the extent permitted by law. The Secretary shall issue new policy guidance to all Department of Homeland Security personnel regarding the appropriate and consistent use of lawful detention authority under the INA, including the termination of the practice commonly known as "catch and release," whereby aliens are routinely released in the United States shortly after their apprehension for violations of immigration law.

Sec. 7. Return to Territory. The Secretary shall take appropriate action, consistent with the requirements of section 1232 of title 8, United States Code, to ensure that aliens described in section 235(b)(2)(C) of the INA (8 U.S.C. 1225(b)(2)(C)) are returned to the territory from which they came pending a formal removal proceeding.

Sec. 8. Additional Border Patrol Agents. Subject to available appropriations, the Secretary, through the Commissioner of U.S. Customs and Border Protection, shall take all appropriate action to hire 5,000 additional Border Patrol agents, and all appropriate action to ensure that such agents enter on duty and are assigned to duty stations as soon as is practicable.

Sec. 9. Foreign Aid Reporting Requirements. The head of each executive department and agency shall identify and quantify all sources of direct and indirect Federal aid or assistance to the Government of Mexico on an annual basis over the past five years, including all bilateral and multilateral development aid, economic assistance, humanitarian aid, and military aid. Within 30 days of the date of this order, the head of each executive department and agency shall submit this information to the Secretary of State.

Within 60 days of the date of this order, the Secretary shall submit to the President a consolidated report reflecting the levels of such aid and assistance that has been provided annually, over each of the past five years.

Sec. 10. Federal-State Agreements. It is the policy of the executive branch to empower State and local law enforcement agencies across the country to perform the functions of an immigration officer in the interior of the United States to the maximum extent permitted by law.

(a) In furtherance of this policy, the Secretary shall immediately take appropriate action to engage with the Governors of the States, as well as local officials, for the purpose of preparing to enter into agreements under section 287(g) of the INA (8 U.S.C. 1357(g)).

(b) To the extent permitted by law, and with the consent of State or local officials, as appropriate, the Secretary shall take appropriate action, through agreements under section 287(g) of the INA, or otherwise, to authorize State and local law enforcement officials, as the Secretary determines are qualified and appropriate, to perform the functions of immigration officers in relation to the investigation, apprehension, or detention of aliens in the United States under the direction and the supervision of the Secretary. Such authorization shall be in addition to, rather than in place of, Federal performance of these duties.

(c) To the extent permitted by law, the Secretary may structure each agreement under section 287(g) of the INA in the manner that provides the most effective model for enforcing Federal immigration laws and obtaining operational control over the border for that jurisdiction.

Sec. 11. Parole, Asylum, and Removal. It is the policy of the executive branch to end the abuse of parole and asylum provisions currently used to prevent the lawful removal of removable aliens.

(a) The Secretary shall immediately take all appropriate action to ensure that the parole and asylum provisions of Federal immigration law are not illegally exploited to prevent the removal of otherwise removable aliens.

(b) The Secretary shall take all appropriate action, including by promulgating any appropriate regulations, to ensure that asylum referrals and credible fear determinations pursuant to section 235(b)(1) of the INA (8 U.S.C. 1125(b)(1)) and 8 CFR 208.30, and reasonable fear determinations pursuant to 8 CFR 208.31, are conducted in a manner consistent with the plain language of those provisions.

(c) Pursuant to section 235(b)(1)(A)(iii)(I) of the INA, the Secretary shall take appropriate action to apply, in his sole and unreviewable discretion, the provisions of section 235(b)(1)(A)(i) and (ii) of the INA to the aliens designated under section 235(b)(1)(A)(iii)(II).

(d) The Secretary shall take appropriate action to ensure that parole authority under section 212(d)(5) of the INA (8 U.S.C. 1182(d)(5)) is exercised only on a case-by-case basis in accordance with the plain language of the statute, and in all circumstances only when an individual demonstrates urgent humanitarian reasons or a significant public benefit derived from such parole.

(e) The Secretary shall take appropriate action to require that all Department of Homeland Security personnel are properly trained on the proper application of section 235 of the William Wilberforce Trafficking Victims Protection Reauthorization Act of 2008 (8 U.S.C. 1232) and section 462(g)(2) of the Homeland Security Act of 2002 (6 U.S.C. 279(g)(2)), to ensure that unaccompanied alien children are properly processed, receive appropriate care and placement while in the custody of the Department of Homeland Security, and, when appropriate, are safely repatriated in accordance with law.

Sec. 12. Authorization to Enter Federal Lands. The Secretary, in conjunction with the Secretary of the Interior and any other heads of agencies as necessary, shall take all appropriate action to:

(a) permit all officers and employees of the United States, as well as all State and local officers as authorized by the Secretary, to have access to all Federal lands as necessary and appropriate to implement this order; and

(b) enable those officers and employees of the United States, as well as all State and local officers as authorized by the Secretary, to perform such actions on Federal lands as the Secretary deems necessary and appropriate to implement this order.

Sec. 13. Priority Enforcement. The Attorney General shall take all appropriate steps to establish prosecution guidelines and allocate appropriate resources to ensure that Federal prosecutors accord a high priority to prosecutions of offenses having a nexus to the southern border.

Sec. 14. Government Transparency. The Secretary shall, on a monthly basis and in a publicly available way, report statistical data on aliens apprehended at or near the southern border using a uniform method of reporting by all Department of Homeland Security components, in a format that is easily understandable by the public.

Sec. 15. Reporting. Except as otherwise provided in this order, the Secretary, within 90 days of the date of this order, and the Attorney General, within 180 days, shall each submit to the President a report on the progress of the directives contained in this order.

Sec. 16. Hiring. The Office of Personnel Management shall take appropriate action as may be necessary to facilitate hiring personnel to implement this order.

Sec. 17. General Provisions.

(a) Nothing in this order shall be construed to impair or otherwise affect:

(i) the authority granted by law to an executive department or agency, or the head thereof; or

(ii) the functions of the Director of the Office of Management and Budget relating to budgetary, administrative, or legislative proposals.

(b) This order shall be implemented consistent with applicable law and subject to the availability of appropriations.

(c) This order is not intended to, and does not, create any right or benefit, substantive or procedural, enforceable at law or in equity by any party against the United States, its departments, agencies, or entities, its officers, employees, or agents, or any other person.

DONALD J. TRUMP
THE WHITE HOUSE,
January 25, 2017.

Practical Reasons Should Motivate the Construction of a Border Wall

Reece Jones

Reece Jones serves as an associate professor and chair of graduate studies in the Department of Geography at the Manoa branch of the University of Hawaii. He authored a book in 2012 titled Border Walls: Security and the War on Terror in the United States, India, and Israel.

We live a world of borders and walls. In addition to the massive and expensive barrier on long stretches of the U.S.-Mexico border, in the 23 years since the fall of the Berlin Wall, 26 other new walls and fences have gone up on political borders around the world. These walls are built by both totalitarian regimes and democracies, including India, Thailand, Israel, South Africa, and the European Union. Invariably, the barriers are justified in the language of security—the country must be protected from the terrorists, drug cartels, insurgents, or suicide bombers lurking on the other side.

Despite the external focus of these justifications, in most instances these walls and fences are actually the result of the internal politics of the state that builds them. There are three specific reasons for constructing a border wall: establishing sovereignty over ungoverned or unruly lands; protecting the wealth of the state and population; and protecting cultural practices within the state from the possible influence of other value systems possessed by immigrants. The decision to build the 664-mile barrier along the U.S.-Mexico border, although often presented as primarily in response to drug-related violence and terrorism, is largely due to these internal factors.

The desire to establish clear sovereign authority over the state's territory is the first factor that underlies the construction of a

"Why Build a Border Wall?" by Reece Jones, Nacla. Reprinted by permission.

border barrier. Although we often imagine the territorial outline of countries as sharply drawn lines where the control of one state ends and another begins, most borders on the ground belie this simplicity. The idea that borders (or rivers or coastlines) are lines is a convenience of cartography that is established on the ground many years after a map is drawn, if at all. The oldest political borders in Europe, for example, are only a few hundred years old, and most were established more recently than that. Before the 1600s, most states did not recognize each other's sovereign authority over a territory, and the technological advances in cartography that allowed fixed borders and territories to be represented had not been achieved. Consequently, even the simple idea that states have clearly defined territories that are marked by a linear border is a very recent development.

The contemporary U.S.-Mexico border was established on maps at the end of the U.S.-Mexican War by the Treaty of Guadalupe Hidalgo.[1] The war settled which territories the expansion-minded United States could claim and transferred almost half of Mexico's territory to the United States. The last sections of the border were finalized with the Gadsden Purchase in 1854, which secured mining rights and a better route for a railroad connection to California. At the time, the territory was part of the United States in name only and, despite the enormous land area, was populated by about 100,000 Mexicans and 200,000 Native Americans.[2] Over the intervening years, sovereign authority over these lands was established by moving Anglo populations onto the land and by violently suppressing any resistance. Land surveying, creating property maps, and the deployment of police forces resignified the landscape. Yet the line existed on the map and in the population's geographic imagination only inchoately, as the practices and performances of sovereignty slowly inscribed the different territories onto the landscape.

This process accelerated in the 1990s as funding for border security increased substantially and the idea of marking the imagined line with a physical barrier took hold. When the Border Patrol was established in 1924, it was tiny and remained underfunded for decades. In 1992, there were 3,555 agents at the U.S.-Mexico border, but by 2010 there were over 20,100.[3] These changes have both practical and symbolic effects on the hardening of the border. The additional agents play a practical enforcement role while the fence project, which passed Congress in 2006, is much more symbolically significant. Walls and fences are the most efficient way to mark territorial differences on the ground because they take the abstract idea of a territory and materialize it. The construction of the barrier is another step in the process of reimaging these formerly Native American and Mexican lands as firmly part of the territory of the United States. By physically inscribing the line in the landscape, the wall brings the border into being and visually demonstrates where U.S. territory ends and Mexican territory begins.

The second internal factor that results in the construction of a wall or fence on a border is the presence of a poorer country on the other side. In previous eras, political borders served primarily as either military defensive lines where one army prevented the movement of another or as markers of different government regimes where one set of laws and taxes or one cultural system stopped and another began. Over the 20th century, the practice of absolute sovereignty over a bounded territory produced substantial wealth inequalities globally, which increased the desire of many people to move either to avoid deteriorating conditions in their home state or to seek better economic opportunities elsewhere.[4] These movements, along with the possibility of hostile people or items passing into the state, resulted in a much more substantial focus on borders as a location to prevent the unauthorized movement of people.

Just as we often imagine most borders as the sharp lines depicted on maps, we also imagine that historically most borders were fenced and fortified, but this is not the case. The older purposes of borders as defensive military lines or administrative divisions do not necessitate a wall or fence. Fences do not deter tanks and airplanes, and administrative divisions between peaceful neighbors do not require an expensive barrier. The changing purpose for borders is evident in the sheer number of new barriers built in the past 20 years. Twenty-seven have been built since 1998, compared with 11 during the entire Cold War period from 1945 until 1990. Furthermore, several of those Cold War barriers were quite short including the U.S. fence with Cuba at Guantánamo Bay and the fence between Gibraltar and Spain.

Not only are the new barriers longer than in the past, but many are built along peaceful borders. The significant characteristic that most of these borders share is that they mark a sharp wealth discontinuity.[5] For example, the average annual per capita GDP (in 2010 U.S. dollars) of the countries that have built barriers since the fall of the Berlin Wall is $14,067; the average for the countries on the other side of these barriers is $2,801. The U.S. barrier on the Mexican border fits this pattern. Although the Canadian border is longer and certainly more porous (the Border Patrol estimated in 2009 that it had effective control over less than 1% of the Canadian border versus 35% of the Mexican border), the debates about fencing the border focused only on Mexico.[6] The United States' per capita GDP in 2010 was $47,000, Canada's was $39,000, and Mexico's was $14,000.

The final internal factor that plays a role in the decision to build a fence or wall on a political border is the fear that population movements will irreversibly change the way of life inside the state. In the United States, concerns about the threat that immigrant values pose are as old as the country itself. At different points in history, the Irish, the Chinese, and the Italians were all described as posing a grave threat to a particular version of what it meant to be an "American." Today, these debates revolve around both Muslims and Latino immigrants who, anti-immigrant activists argue, bring alternative social codes and do not assimilate into the mainstream of U.S. society. The fence on the border symbolizes the hardened and fixed borderline that marks a clear distinction between the territories where particular people belong.

The construction of a barrier on the border simultaneously legitimates and intensifies the internal exclusionary practices of the sovereign state. It legitimates exclusion by providing a material manifestation of the abstract idea of sovereignty, which brings the claim of territorial difference into being. The barrier also intensifies these exclusionary practices, because once the boundary is marked and "the container" of the state takes form, the perception of the difference between the two places becomes stronger. This process is evident in new restrictive immigration laws at the state level in Alabama and Arizona as well as in the protests and vandalism directed toward proposed Islamic cultural centers in New York and Tennessee. By demonstrating sovereign control, the state simultaneously reifies authority over that territory and defines the limits of the people that belong there. These perceived differences then fuel more passionate feelings of belonging to the in-group and distinction from the other on the outside.

The U.S. fence on the Mexican border should be understood both in terms of the enhanced enforcement capabilities of the government and in the assertion of where the state has authority and who should be allowed in the state's territory. The United States built the barrier on the U.S.-Mexico border to define its sovereign authority over its territory, to protect the economic privileges of its population, and to protect a particular way of life from other people who are perceived to have different value systems. Rather than a barrier against terrorism and cartel violence, it is a performance of the United States' territory and boundaries.

Endnotes

1. Joseph Werne, *The Imaginary Line: A History of the United States and Mexican Boundary Survey*, 1848–57 (Texas Christian University Press, 2007).

2. Joseph Nevins, *Operation Gatekeeper and Beyond: The War on "Illegals" and the Remaking of the US-Mexico Boundary* (Routledge, 2010), 26–8; Kelly Lytle Hernández, Migra! A History of the US Border Patrol (University of California Press, 2010), 21–2.

3. Chad C. Haddal, *Border Security: The Role of the Border Patrol* (Washington DC: Congressional Research Services, 2010), 13.

4. John Agnew, *Globalization and Sovereignty* (Rowman & Littlefield, 2009), 1–45; Richard E. Baldwin, Phillip Martin, and Gianmarco Ottaviano, "Global Income Divergence, Trade, and Industrialization: The Geography of Growth Take-Offs." Journal of Economic Growth 6, no. 1 (2001): 5–37.

5. Stéphane Rosière and Reece Jones, "Teichopolitics: Reconsidering Globalization Through the Role of Walls and Fences," *Geopolitics* 17, no. 1 (2012): 217–34.

6. Todd Owen, Congressional Testimony, House Oversight and Government Reform Committee (July 9, 2009), 3.

The United States Can Benefit from Building a Different Wall in Mexico

David North

David North is a Fellow of the Center for Immigration Studies and a widely recognized authority on immigration policy. His focus is interaction between immigration and domestic systems, such as education and labor markets.

Amidst all the high-decibel and highly generalized discussions of our southern border,

We're going to do a wall ... Mexico's going to pay for the wall. — The Donald

A person who thinks only about building walls, wherever they may be, and not building bridges, is not Christian. — The Pope

Let us make a highly specific, extremely cost-effective, low-decibel (if politically unlikely) proposal about stemming the flow of illegal migrants from Central America.

The suggestion is based on three quite separate, but mutually supporting sets of facts.

Fact One

While illegal migration from Mexico remains a major problem, that nation's developing middle-class economy, and the lowering of birth rates over the last two decades, means that the illegal migration from that country is plateauing.

"How About a Wall in Mexico That We Pay For?" by David North, The Center for Immigration Studies, February 24, 2016. Reprinted by permission.

Meanwhile, illegal migration through Mexico from Central America has exploded, largely because while the administration is perfectly willing to expel 17- and 18-year-old Mexican nationals arriving illegally, it will not do the same to those from Central America. And the economic situation in Central America now is grim—it is roughly comparable to what it was in Mexico 30 years ago.

Fact Two

Our essentially non-Hispanic government has, at least currently, major hesitations about discouraging the migration of Hispanics, but the all-Hispanic government of Mexico has no similar hang-ups about enforcing migration laws against other Hispanic populations. Further, the executive branch there is far less likely to be inhibited by the courts, or by the concept of political correctness, than ours is.

In short, Mexico is exactly the right place to enforce immigration law on non-Mexican law-breakers. This is something than can be done, given the right incentives.

Fact Three

Then there is the matter of geography. Mexico is at its broadest at its 1,900-mile-long northern border with the United States, and that is where we try to enforce our immigration law. Mexico is at its narrowest, as the map shows, near its own southeastern border. The distance from the Gulf of Mexico to the Pacific, as the crow flies, is 130 or so miles. This is the Isthmus of Tehuantepec; all land-borne illegal migration from Central America flows through this relatively narrow choke-point.

The Little Railway that Might

Given these three facts would it not make sense to pay Mexico to cut off the northward-migration of Central Americans? To some extent that is happening now, but our proposal is to make it more effective and easier to manage and monitor.

The suggestion is to construct a fence along an existing railroad, now nearly abandoned, built by dreamers a little more than 100 years ago who thought that they could entice ocean-to-ocean traffic away from the about-to-be built Panama Canal and across the Isthmus of Tehuantepec instead. The dream became a nightmare when it became apparent that using the canal was cheaper and faster than unloading freight at the Gulf of Mexico end of the little railway, shipping it by rail, and then re-loading it on ships at the Pacific end of the line. One website calls it the "UnPanama."

The railway bears the Spanish initials FIT (Ferrocarril del Istmo de Tehuantepec). It runs from sea to sea in a seamless line, though not in a straight line, so it's about 190 miles long. There is a gap in the mountains at this point, which made the rail line easier to build and to maintain. Since the Isthmus is running east and west at this point, the railroad runs roughly north (the Gulf of Mexico) to south (the Pacific).

Our notion is to build a strong pedestrian fence on the western side of the route, allowing Mexican officials to use the rail line, and roads parallel to it, to patrol it. This would be a much better design than fences at our southern border, because if they are built right at the border, our Border Patrol has no power to seize people approaching it from the other side, as they are in another country.

There would have to be several places in the proposed fence, maybe a dozen or so, where legitimate crossings could take place, essentially from one part of Mexico to another. These crossings would be staffed by Mexican officials (presumably paid indirectly with U.S. funds). These crossing guards, the construction workers needed to build the fence, and the patrol agents would represent a huge economic shot in the arm for the state of Oaxaca, which is the second-poorest of all Mexican states. (The northern part of the line is in Veracruz state, which is also relatively poor.) The line would also be a few miles to the west of the state of Chiapas, the poorest of the Mexican states.

What about the Railway?

The railway is still operating, but barely, as my colleague Kausha Luna learned after a number of phone calls. It is a single track (which suggests it never had much business); it currently carries some freight, but no passengers; and is owned by a government corporation, perhaps like our Amtrak (which is another clue to its lack of prosperity). Further, it was heavily damaged in a 2005 hurricane.

Up until nine years ago, the right to operate the line was in the hands of an American firm, the Genesee & Wyoming, which is a conglomerate of short lines headquartered in Connecticut. In 2007 the G&W opted out of this arrangement, at least party because of the storm. Then the rail line itself, and many other miles of railroad, were sold to a government-related entity at a bargain price.

The FIT railway, thus, cannot be worth much at the moment. Ideally the line would not run trains anymore, leaving the Mexican police free to use the rails to enforce their immigration law, free of complications made by the occasional freight train. Perhaps that could be arranged at a reasonable price.

The relative ease of the construction of a fence along the FIT railway, as opposed to along the U.S. southern border, is hard to overemphasize. Here is a relatively level land route in which the railway already owns all the real estate needed for the fence. The railway itself gives instant access to the area where the fence is to be built. Construction costs in Mexico are much lower in Mexico than in the States. There would be not be ranches along the border, as there are on some segments of our southern border, where part of the land would be one side of the fence, and part on the other. The railway follows a much straighter line than the Rio Grande, and so forth.

Above all, the total length would be just one-tenth the length of our border with Mexico. This is not to suggest that we abandon efforts to strengthen our own southern border, but the FIT fence would be an extremely valuable tool in the American enforcement arsenal.

There would be problems, of course. One of them would be the politics of building a barrier right in the middle of another nation, but with the price of oil lower than it has been in a long time, Mexico might be lured into the deal because of Uncle Sam's money. Such a barrier would also help Mexico control its own illegal immigration problems, all at the cost of another nation.

Then there would be the problem of controlling corruption among the involved Mexican officials, and seeing to it that the new fence was doing what it is supposed to do.

The Pope would not like the idea, but given a Trump presidency (I shudder at the prospect) perhaps The Donald would see this as an inexpensive and effective way to honor a campaign pledge.

Trump's Wall Is Implausible from an Engineering Perspective

Ali F. Rhuzkan

Ali F. Rhuzkan is the pen name of a professional engineer and amateur writer who works in New York City.

There are very few occasions in American political discourse that require the input of a structural engineer, but when Donald Trump took a question from Univision's Jorge Ramos regarding his proposed United States-Mexico border wall at a press conference on August 25, I heard the clarion call:

> RAMOS: How are you going to build a 1,900-mile wall?
> TRUMP: Very easy. I'm a builder. That's easy. I build buildings that are—can I tell you what's more complicated? What's more complicated is building a building that's 95 stories tall. Okay?

No. Donald Trump is not a builder. Donald Trump could not build a doghouse. Donald Trump is a developer who pays what he would call "very, very smart people" to build things on his behalf. His response to Ramos' question was meant both to exaggerate his understanding of construction and to downplay the challenges posed by his border wall project.

Though I would never classify the construction of a 95-story building as *simple*, it is a feat that has been achieved many times before. There are at least 30 buildings that have reached a height of 95 stories or more, according to the obsessively detailed database at SkyscraperPage.com, and there are even more in the design phase or under construction.

On the other hand, human beings have built a 2,000-mile-long frontier wall exactly one time. Once. And it was accomplished only through a centuries-long building campaign that necessitated the forced labor of millions of Chinese peasants.

"An Engineer Explains Why Trump's Wall Is So Implausible," by Ali F. Rhuzkan, The National Memo, September 21, 2015. Reprinted by permission.

The challenge of Trump's border wall is not technical, but logistical. The leap in complexity between "building a wall" and "building a 2,000-mile-long continuous border wall in the desert" is about equal to the gap between "killing a guy" and "waging a protracted land war." Trump's border wall, if built as he has described it, would be one of the largest civil works projects in the history of the country and would face an array of challenges not found when constructing 95-story skyscrapers.

In order to adequately answer Mr. Ramos' question, let's first make some assumptions on the project's scope: A successful border wall must be effective, cheap, and easily maintained. It should be built from readily available materials and should take advantage of the capabilities of the existing labor force. The wall should reach about five feet underground to deter tunneling, and should terminate about 20 feet above grade to deter climbing.

To be classified as a "wall" rather than a "fence," the barrier must also be a continuous, non-porous construction. This distinction might seem purely semantic, but Trump has made himself very clear on the matter, saying, "A wall is better than fencing, and it's much more powerful. It's more secure. It's taller." So we'll take him at his word: He wants to build a *wall*.

One of the biggest choices that a builder has to make is what material to use for his or her project. For Trump's wall, I would first dismiss concrete masonry unit (commonly called cinderblock) construction because each block would have to be put in place and set in mortar by hand. The finished product would probably be acceptable, but construction would be outrageously labor intensive and therefore costly.

Next, I would dismiss steel wire mesh. While it is cheap and readily available, it can be easily penetrated by a pair of wire cutters, an angle grinder, an oxy-acetylene torch, or just a Chevy going really fast. Even though extant barrier sections along the border make use of wire mesh, the United States Border Patrol is constantly battling to repair breaches and, as stated above, this kind of barrier really falls into the category of "fence."

That leaves concrete. A concrete wall would meet all of the basic project requirements, and as a bonus would also embody the gray-faced antipathy of America's immigration policy. There are two major types of concrete construction:

- cast-in-place, where wet, plastic concrete is brought in trucks to a job site, cast into formwork, and then cured; and
- pre-cast concrete, where the concrete is cast in a controlled indoor environment, cured, and then shipped to the construction site for assembly.

The hot, dry climate in the border regions would complicate cast-in-place construction because high heat tends to screw up the chemical reactions that cause concrete to harden.

I drew up a quick design option for a pre-cast concrete wall, not dissimilar to many proprietary systems currently on the market. This design consists of I-shaped concrete columns spaced at 10 feet on center, with eight-inch-thick wall panels spanning in between them. In such a design, the only concrete that would need to be cast on site would be for the foundations. The columns would anchored to the foundations, and the wall panels are slipped in place from above.

If we assume a border wall length of 1,954 miles (there are 600 or so miles of existing border barrier, but much of this would not qualify for Trump's wall), then we can make some estimates as to the volume of concrete needed for the project:

- Foundation: 6 feet deep, 18 inch radius = 42.4 cubic feet
- Column: 4 square feet area by 30 feet tall = 120 cubic feet
- Wall panels: 25 feet tall by 10 feet long by 8 inches thick = 166.7 cubic feet
- Total concrete per 10-foot segment = 329.1 cubic feet
- 1,954 miles = 10,300,00 feet = 1,030,000 segments (10-feet long each)

- 1,030,000 segments * 329.1 cubic feet per segment = 339,000,000 cubic feet = 12,555,000 cubic yards. (The cubic yard is the standard unit of measure of concrete volume in the United States.)

Twelve million, six hundred thousand cubic yards. In other words, this wall would contain over three times the amount of concrete used to build the Hoover Dam—a project that, unlike Trump's wall, has qualitative, verifiable economic benefits.

Such a wall would be greater in volume than all six pyramids of the Giza Necropolis—and it is unlikely that a concrete slab in the town of Dead Dog Valley, Texas would inspire the same timeless sense of wonder.

That quantity of concrete could pave a one-lane road from New York to Los Angeles, going the long way around the Earth, which would probably be just as useful.

Concrete, of course, requires reinforcing steel (or rebar). A reasonable estimate for the amount of rebar would be about 3 percent of the total wall size, resulting in a steel volume of 10,190,000 cubic feet, or about 5 billion pounds. We could melt down 4 of our Nimitz-class aircraft carriers and would probably be a few cruisers short of having enough steel.

But the challenge is far greater than simply collecting the necessary raw materials. All of these hundreds of miles of wall would need to be cast in concrete facilities, probably project-specific ones that have been custom built near the border. Then, the pre-cast wall pieces would need to be shipped by truck through the inhospitable, often roadless desert.

The men and women doing the work of actually installing the wall would have to be provided with food, water, shelter, lavatory facilities, safety equipment, transportation, and medical care, and would sometimes be miles away from a population center of any size. Sure, some people would be willing to to do the work, but at what price? Would Trump hire Mexicans?

This analysis also ignores the less sexy aspects of large-scale engineering projects: surveying, land acquisition, environmental review, geological studies, maintenance, excavating for foundations, and so on. Theoretical President Trump may be able to executive-order his way through the laser grid of lawsuits that normally impede this kind of work, but he can't ignore the physical realities of construction.

Trump's border wall is not impossible, but it would certainly be a more challenging endeavor than he would ever lead you to believe. Maybe he should stick to 95-story buildings.

A Wall Would Cause Harm to the Environment

Shonil Bhagwat

Shonil Bhagwat is an environmental geographer with broad research interests at the cross-section between natural and social sciences. He is senior lecturer in geography at the Open University, a world leader in modern distance learning.

I t looks like Donald Trump's "great, great wall" is actually going to happen. Its likely impact on human society has been well-noted, but in the longer-term a barrier across an entire continent will also have severe ecological consequences.

The US-Mexico border is around 1,900 miles (3,100 km) long and some of it has already been fenced off. According to Trump the proposed wall will cover approximately 1,000 miles and "natural obstacles" such as rivers or mountains will take care of the rest.

Aside from the debates over whether or not the wall will do much to stop drug trafficking or illegal immigration, how much it will cost the US taxpayer, or whether Mexico will pay for it, a 1,000-mile wall has significant environmental costs. For a start, all that concrete will generate millions of tons of carbon dioxide emissions. And then you have the fact the wall will ravage a unique desert habitat that straddles the two countries and will prevent the movement of local animals.

US Fish & Wildlife Service (FWS) has estimated that the wall will threaten 111 endangered species as it passes through four key wildlife reserves on the US side of the border and several nature reserves on the Mexican side.

Some of the affected species are obvious: animals with cross-border populations include bighorn sheep, ocelots and bears.

Splitting plant and animal populations by building a concrete wall promotes inbreeding and a decrease in genetic diversity, which makes many species susceptible to diseases and epidemics. The wall is also likely to wipe out the few jaguars still lingering in Arizona and New Mexico by cutting them off from breeding populations south of the border.

Other species are more unexpected: the bald eagle, America's national bird, can obviously fly over any barriers yet the disruption to its habitat means it makes the FWS's list of affected migratory birds. Even marine animals such as manatees or sea turtles can't escape the wall's impact.

Long division

The Trump wall may never become anything more solid than a metaphor for increased border surveillance, aided by technology, to keep illegal immigration under control. However, if a vast concrete wall really is built, and if it is as tall and impenetrable as Trump hopes, it will presumably last for thousands of years. This will have long-term ecological consequences.

The glacial and interglacial cycles of ice ages and warm periods unfold over thousands of years. Over the past 11,000 years we have had a relatively stable climate, but anthropogenic warming is delaying the arrival of the next ice age.

As species start to feel the pressure of a warming climate, they will need to move towards the poles as their habitats shift. Plants and animals currently found in central Mexico may find their "natural" home moves north of the border. The wall will make such movement impossible and will make these species vulnerable to the effects of climate change.

Equally, in the much longer term, if or when the next ice age eventually begins and ice sheets start to expand southwards, species from the north of the wall will need to move south to escape the freezing temperatures. The Trump wall will pose a significant obstacle for such movements.

On evolutionary timescales of millions of years, such an obstacle in the movement of animals and plants will drive extinctions and the emergence of new species. A political act of this kind can have far-reaching consequences for the ecological and even evolutionary landscapes.

Build bridges instead

Preexisting security barriers across the US-Mexico border are already making life difficult for local wildlife, according to peer-reviewed research.

Scientists across the world consistently call for more permeable border fences in order to allow animals to move through them. One 2011 study even looked specifically at the US-Mexico border. The authors warned species were being forced into risky unfenced "bottlenecks" and called for better planning tailored towards wildlife movement.

Our knowledge of how to conserve animals across international borders has come a long way. Many nations have embraced shared responsibility for shared wildlife, and a number of international legal instruments also set out the "dos and don'ts" for conservation in transboundary regions.

If Trump really wants to show his prowess in construction, and wants to leave a long-term infrastructure legacy, then he should build bridges for wildlife on the US-Mexico border—not walls.

Are There More Effective Ways to Prevent Illegal Immigration?

Overview: Border Security Is a Question of Management

Caitlin Cruz

Caitlin Cruz is a magazine reporter and essayist. She was a digital reporter at Cronkite News and has written about national affairs and the 2016 election for Talking Points Memo.

The Akwesasne Mohawk Indian Territory occupies a unique position on the U.S.-Canada border.

That is evident as Akwesasne Mohawk Police Chief Jerry Swamp points to a small island behind his police station that, because of the March snow, almost blends into the St. Lawrence River. At a point next to the island, multiple jurisdictions collide. New York state and two Canadian provinces, Ontario and Quebec, come together there, and the Akwesasne territory sits on top of it all. Law enforcement officials from multiple national, state and local agencies patrol the area. The boundaries are a byproduct of the settlement of the War of 1812.

"Just so happened that the borders were imposed upon our community right in the middle," said Swamp.

Like border communities to the south, the Akwesasne territory is dealing with drugs, smuggling, jurisdictional overlap and the question of what constitutes a secure border.

"Because we are a border community, we have a lot of the same issues that pretty much any other border community has between U.S. and Canada, probably as well as the southern border between U.S. and Mexico," said Swamp, a 22-year police force veteran.

But as Congress struggles with questions of border security and immigration reform, it's really a tale of one border, not two, that is being debated.

Security North and South

Despite the fact that the border between the mainland United States and Canada is twice as long as the border between the U.S. and Mexico, the focus in Congress is all on the southwest. The numbers tell why.

The U.S. Border Patrol reported that in the fiscal year ending Sept. 30, 2012, agents apprehended 356,873 undocumented immigrants along the 1,969-mile border with Mexico. By contrast, along the 3,987-mile Canadian border, they arrested 4,210.

During the same time frame, Border Patrol agents at the southern border confiscated nearly 2.3 million pounds of marijuana and 12,160 pounds of cocaine. In the north, agents seized 1,542 of marijuana and 206 pounds of cocaine.

It's disparities like those that could eventually dominate the debate about how the United States will deem either border "secure" and how it will deal with the unabated flow of drugs and illegal immigrants.

The comprehensive immigration bill passed by the Senate and languishing in the House of Representatives would more than double the number of Border Patrol agents from the current 18,576 at the southern border to nearly 38,000 and add 3,500 customs agents at ports of entry nationwide. By contrast, only 2,206 Border Patrol agents currently are stationed along the Canadian border.

The bill would add another 700 miles of fencing between the U.S. and Mexico, roughly doubling again the level of current fencing. The Canadian border has virtually no fencing and is often referred to as the largest unguarded border in the world.

The Senate measure would also vastly expand the use of drones to patrol the southern border, as well as other high-tech surveillance equipment. And it would require an exit monitoring system at air and sea ports of entry, in recognition of the fact that up to 40 percent of the 11.2 million undocumented immigrants in the U.S. came here legally and overstayed their visas. However, there is no provision or plan for tracking down visa overstayers.

The projected cost of those and other security measures is $46.3 billion.

Defining, Measuring Border Security

Still, those who live along the border and know it best say if the goal is to block anyone from sneaking across the border, all the spending still won't work.

"I don't care who says what," said Arturo R. Garino, the mayor of Nogales, Ariz., and a former police officer. "The border will never be fully secured, unless we were to build a wall like Berlin, and even then it wasn't secured."

At the northern border, New York Erie County Undersheriff Mark N. Wipperman echoes the sentiment.

"We don't get the numbers or see the numbers the south border does," said Wipperman. "But it only takes one individual with bad intentions to do a lot of damage."

Audrey Macklin, a professor of law at the University of Toronto who specializes in border and immigration issues, said both the northern and southern borders are too vast for traditional methods of enforcement such as fences or extra boots on the ground.

"I think governments are committed to perpetuating the idea that sovereignty … is how effectively one can regulate the movement of each and every individual across the border at each and every location along the border," said Macklin, who has law degrees from Yale and the University of Toronto. "That's a naive view of sovereignty and border control. But no government feels that it can afford to tell the population of their countries that [idea] is naive, futile and unattainable."

Macklin instead suggests border management.

"Border management can be real, but border management requires an admission that borders are by their very nature porous," she said. "They can never be hermetically sealed. Countries wouldn't even want to do what is necessary to hermetically seal them because their economies would collapse."

Border enforcement spending over the past decade in the U.S. hasn't come close to shutting down illegal immigration and drug smuggling. But stepped-up enforcement, coupled with a lagging job market in the U.S. and an improving economy in Mexico, has slowed immigration to the point that demographers say there is "net zero" immigration. In other words, just as many people from Mexico are leaving the U.S. as coming in and illegal immigration is at its lowest point in decades.

But to get to that point, the growth in border security spending has been exponential. At the end of fiscal year 2004, the Department of Homeland Security, which oversees the Border Patrol and Customs and Border Protection, had about 28,100 personnel assigned to patrol land and sea borders and ports of entry nationwide at a cost of about $5.9 billion.

By the end of fiscal year 2011, those numbers increased to 41,400 personnel at a cost of $11.8 billion.

And according to a report by the Migration Policy Institute, the U.S. spent $18 billion on immigration enforcement in fiscal 2012, $4 billion more than all of the other federal law enforcement agencies combined, including the Federal Bureau of Investigation and the Drug Enforcement Administration.

Yet, with all the spending, the Government Accountability Office, the investigative arm of Congress, reported in 2010 that less than half—44 percent—of the southwestern border was under "operational control." That is approximately 866 miles of unsecure border.

At the Canadian border, the situation is much worse. In February 2011, the GAO found only 69 miles of the northern border—or 1.25 percent of the entire U.S.-Canada border—to be under operational control.

Those figures are important because they indicate how much enforcement has to be stepped up to meet requirements in the Senate immigration reform bill now pending in Congress. The bill changes terminology from seeking "operational control" to requiring "effective control in high risk border sectors along the Southern Border."

An analysis by the Immigration Policy Center, the research arm of the American Immigration Council, which promotes America's history as a nation of immigrants, indicates the new standards are much tougher than the levels of security that currently have been reached. The analysis says the Senate's bill defines "effective control" as "persistent surveillance of 100 percent of the border and a 90 percent effectiveness rate in preventing illegal crossings."

Enforcement is particularly difficult in high-risk sectors like Arizona. According to the Customs and Border Protection fact sheet, "approximately half of all drugs seized and illegal immigrants apprehended entering the United States are seized or apprehended in Arizona."

Quantifying what can be considered a secure border is difficult even for law enforcement veterans like Santa Cruz County Sheriff's Sgt. Rafael Corrales, who has lived all of his life in the Arizona county that shares 50 miles of border with Mexico.

"If by secure you mean safe and there's no drugs or any crime being committed around it, then it's not secure," said Corrales, who has spent 18 years with the sheriff's office. "To me, that would mean no crime, in general, no crime, that we're all safe. That's just my opinion, though."

Corrales' boss, Santa Cruz County Sheriff Tony Estrada, said that even with stepped-up enforcement, both legal and illegal movement will always be a part of the southwestern border.

"This is going to continue to be an active border," said Estrada, who has served as sheriff since 1993. "As long as we have poverty in the world and as long as they're looking at the United States as a place they can make an honest living and have a future for themselves people are (going to) keep coming."

Economic Cooperation Part of the Solution

Estrada believes it will take more than a tougher enforcement strategy to address the border issues.

"I've always said the United States took their eye off Mexico for too long," said Estrada. "They took Mexico for granted for too long. We're joined at the hip just like Canada, and they ignored Mexico."

Through their Beyond the Border pact announced on Feb. 4, 2011, the U.S. and Canada sought to secure the border through trade agreements.

A commitment like Beyond the Border between U.S. and Mexico could be a turning point for the southwestern border, according to Estrada.

"If the U.S. can recognize the potential that Mexico has and explore that or expand it or take advantage of it, I think that would go a long way," Estrada said.

Beyond the Border was born more than 17 years after the North American Free Trade Agreement. U.S. President Barack Obama and Canadian Prime Minister Stephen Harper announced the agreement on Feb. 4, 2011, and said it was designed to bring their countries together as "staunch allies, vital economic partners and steadfast friends."

The agreement features four areas of cooperation: addressing threats early; trade facilitation, economic growth, and jobs; integrated cross-border law enforcement; and critical infrastructure and cyber security.

The action plan states: "We recognize that our efforts should accelerate job creation and economic growth through trade facilitation at our borders and contribute directly to the economic security and well-being of both the United States and Canada."

But more than two years after the announcement, the plan has been criticized by citizens of both countries for its slow implementation and because, unlike the North American Free Trade Agreement implemented in 1994, it did not include Mexico.

Increased Border Security in the North

While enforcement efforts on the southern border have grown exponentially, the Department of Homeland Security released its Northern Border Strategy in June of 2012. It shows that the

Border Patrol has increased its northern presence from 340 agents in 2001 to more 2,200 agents in 2012. The number of customs officers at ports of entry increased from 2,721 officers in 2003 to approximately 3,700 officers in 2012.

The Drug Enforcement Administration has also increased its northern border presence.

"If you can smuggle dope back and forth across the border then you can smuggle people back and forth across the border," said Jim Burns, DEA assistant special agent in charge in upstate New York. "So that's one reason why DEA has ramped up its presence along the northern border and I know that's why Homeland Security has ramped up their presence."

A key reason for the uptick in security on the northern border has been the potential for terrorists coming into the United States from the north. That view was reinforced in April 2013 when the Royal Canadian Mounted Police arrested two men who were suspected of receiving support from al Qaeda to conspire and carry out an attack on a VIA railway train. The targeted train travels from the Toronto area to New York.

Some local government officials say they aren't sure that they want more law enforcement presence along the northern border.

"We have such a large number of people coming across and it's such an important part of our tourism industry that this maybe is not the best place to try to find the one out of a million people that represents a threat and keep the other 999,999 waiting," said Niagara Falls, N.Y., Mayor Paul A. Dyster.

A little further to the east, the Akwesasne Territory straddles the U.S.-Canada border. It is 33 square miles and home to 12,000 people descended from various Indian tribes that pre-date European arrival in the Americas. The people of Akwesasne consider their homeland a sovereign nation.

Akwesasne Mohawk Grand Chief Mike Mitchell describes his people's territory with pride, while acknowledging that money generated by drugs, alcohol, guns and smuggling have affected the Akwesasne community.

"Smuggling goes all across, as you probably have found out, right across North America in one form or another," Mitchell said. "Akwesasne, with its complications of multiple jurisdictions, (it is) more prominent here."

But he said he is working to change the lawless, Wild West image of Akwesasne.

"All the things I do every day try to wipe that image out," he said, adding that his people and territory will remain a "target," in spite of strong efforts to protect the community through education and cultural pride.

The island in the river isn't the only place where jurisdictions collide in the Akwesasne territory. Buildings within the territory straddle the border. The front door to the local radio station—CKON-FM—is in Canada, while the backyard is in the United States. This is a fact of life in the territory.

But Mitchell said the Akwesasne people are one community: "We don't let the border affect us."

Opening the Border Would Bring Security

John Lee

John Lee works as an administrator for the Open Borders website. He has written articles expressing passionate viewpoints in favor of liberal immigration laws.

The Associated Press has a great story out on what a "secure" US-Mexico border would look like. It covers perspectives from various stakeholders on border security, with opinions running the gamut from "The border is as secure as it can ever be" to "It's obviously incredibly unsafe." I am not sure if the AP is fairly representing opinions on the border issue, but the reporting of how life on the border has evolved over time is fascinating.

One thing that strikes me in this reporting is how casually drug smugglers/slave traffickers and good-faith immigrants are easily conflated. Is a secure border one where people who want to move contraband goods or human slaves illegally cannot easily enter? Or is it one where well-meaning people can be indefinitely kept at bay for an arbitrary accident of birth? This passage juxtaposes the two quite different situations:

> And nearly all of more than 70 drug smuggling tunnels found along the border since October 2008 have been discovered in the clay-like soil of San Diego and Tijuana, some complete with hydraulic lifts and rail cars. They've produced some of the largest marijuana seizures in U.S. history.
>
> Still, few attempt to cross what was once the nation's busiest corridor for illegal immigration. As he waited for breakfast at a Tijuana migrant shelter, Jose de Jesus Scott nodded toward a roommate who did. He was caught within seconds and badly injured his legs jumping the fence.

Scott, who crossed the border with relative ease until 2006, said he and a cousin tried a three-day mountain trek to San Diego in January and were caught twice. Scott, 31, was tempted to return to his wife and two young daughters near Guadalajara. But, with deep roots in suburban Los Angeles and cooking jobs that pay up to $1,200 a week, he will likely try the same route a third time.

The main thing that strikes me about the previously "unsecure" border near San Diego is that border patrol agents were overwhelmed by a mass of people until more staff and walls were brought to bear. But these masses of people almost certainly were comprised in large part, if not near-entirely, of good-faith immigrants. Smugglers and traffickers merely take advantage of the confusion to sneak in with the immigrants. If the immigrants had a legal path to entry, if they did not have to cross the border unlawfully, the traffickers would be naked without human crowds to hide in. If border security advocates just want to reduce illegal trafficking, demanding "border security" before loosening immigration controls may well be putting the cart before the horse.

Even so, as I've said before, the physical reality of a long border means that human movement across it can never be fully controlled. Demanding totalitarian control as "true border security" is about as unrealistic as, if not even more so than an open borders advocate demanding the abolition of the nation-state.

The AP covers some damning stories of peaceful Americans murdered by drug traffickers in the same breath as it covers someone trying to get to a job in suburban LA. Even if one insists that murdering smugglers and restaurant cooks should be treated identically on account of being born Mexican, it is difficult to see how one can demand that the US border patrol prioritise detaining them both equally. Yet as long as US visa policy makes it near-impossible for most good-faith Mexicans who can find work in the US to do so, the reality of the border means that thousands of Mexicans just looking to work will risk their lives crossing the border, alongside smugglers and murderers.

The more reasonable policy has to be one that will allow US border patrol to focus on catching the most egregious criminals. That means giving the good-faith immigrants a legal channel to enter the US on a reasonable timeframe, reducing the flow of unlawful border crossings. This is not just my opinion, but that of even a former (Republican) US Ambassador to Mexico (emphasis added):

> Tony Garza remembers watching the flow of pedestrian traffic between Brownsville and Matamoros from his father's filling station just steps from the international bridge. He recalls migrant workers crossing the fairway on the 11th hole of a golf course—northbound in the morning, southbound in the afternoon. And **during an annual celebration between the sister cities, no one was asked for their papers at the bridge. People were just expected to go home.**
>
> Garza, a Republican who served as the U.S. ambassador to Mexico from 2002 to 2009, said it's easy to become nostalgic for those times, but he reminds himself that he grew up in a border town of fewer than 50,000 people that has grown into a city of more than 200,000.
>
> The border here is more secure for the massive investment in recent years but feels less safe because the crime has changed, he said. Some of that has to do with transnational criminal organizations in Mexico and some of it is just the crime of a larger city.
>
> **Reform, he said, "would allow you to focus your resources on those activities that truly make the border less safe today."**

It's the view of those sheriffs who places themselves in harm's way to fight those murderers and smugglers (emphasis added):

> Hidalgo County Sheriff Lupe Trevino points out that drug, gun and human smuggling is nothing new to the border. The difference is the attention that the drug-related violence in Mexico has drawn to the region in recent years.
>
> He insists his county, which includes McAllen, is safe. The crime rate is falling, and illegal immigrants account for small numbers in his jail. But asked if the border is "secure," Trevino doesn't hesitate. "Absolutely not."

"When you're busting human trafficking stash houses with 60 to 100 people that are stashed in a two, three-bedroom home for weeks at a time, how can you say you've secured the border?" he said.

Trevino's view, however, is that **those people might not be there if they had a legal path to work in the U.S.**

"Immigration reform is the first thing we have to accomplish before we can say that we have secured the border," he said.

[…]

In Nogales, Sheriff Tony Estrada has a unique perspective on both border security and more comprehensive immigration reform. Born in Nogales, Mexico, Estrada grew up in Nogales, Ariz., after migrating to the U.S. with his parents. He has served as a lawman in the community since 1966.

He blames border security issues not only on the cartels but on the American demand for drugs. Until that wanes, he said, nothing will change. And securing the border, he added, must be a constant, ever-changing effort that blends security and political support—because the effort will never end.

"The drugs are going to keep coming. The people are going to keep coming. The only thing you can do is contain it as much as possible.

"**I say the border is as safe and secure as it can be, but I think people are asking for us to seal the border, and that's unrealistic,**" he said.

Asked why, he said simply: "That's the nature of the border."

Simply put, if you want a secure US-Mexico border, one where law enforcement can focus on rooting out murderers and smugglers, you need open borders. You need a visa regime that lets those looking to feed their families and looking for a better life to enter legally, with a minimum of muss and fuss. When only those who cross the border unlawfully are those who have no good business being in the US, then you can have a secure border.

More Mexicans Are Leaving Than Moving to the US

Ana Gonzalez-Barrera

Ana Gonzalez-Barrera is a senior researcher at the Pew Research Center with an expertise on Mexican migration flows to the United States using the data of both countries.

Overview

More Mexican immigrants have returned to Mexico from the U.S. than have migrated here since the end of the Great Recession, according to a new Pew Research Center analysis of newly available government data from both countries. The same data sources also show the overall flow of Mexican immigrants between the two countries is at its smallest since the 1990s, mostly due to a drop in the number of Mexican immigrants coming to the U.S.

From 2009 to 2014, 1 million Mexicans and their families (including U.S.-born children) left the U.S. for Mexico, according to data from the 2014 Mexican National Survey of Demographic Dynamics (ENADID). U.S. census data for the same period show an estimated 870,000 Mexican nationals left Mexico to come to the U.S., a smaller number than the flow of families from the U.S. to Mexico.

Measuring migration flows between Mexico and the U.S. is challenging because there are no official counts of how many Mexican immigrants enter and leave the U.S. each year. This report uses the best available government data from both countries to estimate the size of these flows. The Mexican data sources—a national household survey, and two national censuses—asked comparable questions about household members' migration to and from Mexico over the five years previous to each survey or census date. In addition, estimates of Mexican migration to the

"More Mexicans Leaving Than Coming to the U.S." Pew Research Center, Washington, DC (November, 2015) http://www.pewhispanic.org/2015/11/19/more-mexicans-leaving-than-coming-to-the-u-s/.

Net Migration from Mexico to the US

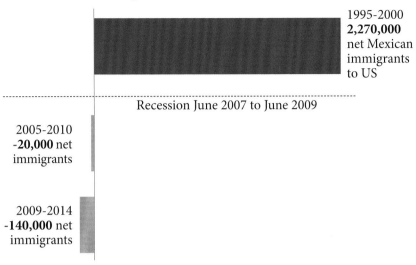

1995-2000
2,270,000
net Mexican
immigrants
to US

Recession June 2007 to June 2009

2005-2010
-20,000 net
immigrants

2009-2014
-140,000 net
immigrants

SOURCE: Pew Research Center

U.S. come from U.S. Census Bureau data, adjusted for undercount, on the number of Mexican immigrants who live in the U.S.

Mexico is the largest birth country among the U.S. foreign-born population—28% of all U.S. immigrants came from there in 2013. Mexico also is the largest source of U.S. unauthorized immigrants (Passel and Cohn, 2014).

The decline in the flow of Mexican immigrants to the U.S. is due to several reasons (Passel et al, 2012). The slow recovery of the U.S. economy after the Great Recession may have made the U.S. less attractive to potential Mexican migrants and may have pushed out some Mexican immigrants as the U.S. job market deteriorated.

In addition, stricter enforcement of U.S. immigration laws, particularly at the U.S.-Mexico border (Rosenblum and Meissner, 2014), may have contributed to the reduction of Mexican immigrants coming to the U.S. in recent years. According to one indicator, U.S. border apprehensions of Mexicans have fallen sharply, to just 230,000 in fiscal year 2014—a level not seen since 1971 (Krogstad and Passel, 2014). At the same time, increased enforcement in the U.S. has led to an increase in the number of Mexican immigrants who have been deported from the U.S. since 2005 (U.S. Department of Homeland Security, 2014).

A majority of the 1 million who left the U.S. for Mexico between 2009 and 2014 left of their own accord, according to the Mexican government's ENADID survey data. The Mexican survey also showed that six in ten (61%) return migrants—those who reported they had been living in the U.S. five years earlier but as of 2014 were back in Mexico—cited family reunification as the main reason for their return. By comparison, 14% of Mexico's return migrants said the reason for their return was deportation from the U.S.

Mexican Immigrant Population in the US, in Millions

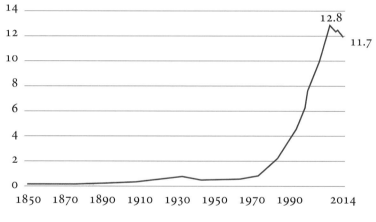

SOURCE: Pew Research Center

Mexican immigrants have been at the center of one of the largest mass migrations in modern history. Between 1965 and 2015 more than 16 million Mexican immigrants migrated to the United States—more than from any other country (Pew Research Center, 2015). In 1970, fewer than 1 million Mexican immigrants lived in the U.S. By 2000, that number had grown to 9.4 million, and by 2007 it reached a peak at 12.8 million. Since then, the Mexican-born population has declined, falling to 11.7 million in 2014, as the number of new arrivals to the U.S. from Mexico declined significantly (Passel et al., 2012); meanwhile the reverse flow to Mexico from the U.S. is now higher.

The decline in the number of Mexican immigrants residing in the U.S. has been mostly due to a drop of more than 1 million unauthorized immigrants from Mexico from a peak of 6.9 million in 2007 to an estimated 5.6 million in 2014 (Passel and Cohn, 2014).

Calculating the Flow from the U.S. to Mexico
To calculate estimates of how many people left the U.S. for Mexico, this report uses data from the 2014 Mexican National Survey of Demographic Dynamics, or ENADID and the 2010 and 2000 Mexican decennial censuses. Each asked all respondents where they had been living five years prior to the date when the survey or census was taken. The answers to this question provide an estimated count of the number of people who moved from the U.S. to Mexico during the five years prior to the survey date. A separate question targets more recent emigrants—people who left Mexico. It asks whether anyone from the household had left for another country during the previous five years; if so, additional questions are asked about whether and when that person or people came back and their reasons for returning to Mexico.

To calculate estimates of how many Mexicans left Mexico for the U.S., this report also uses U.S. Census Bureau's American Community Survey (2005-2013) and the Current Population Survey (2000-2014), both adjusted for undercount, which ask immigrants living the U.S. their country of birth and the year of their arrival in the U.S.

The View From Mexico

The drop in the number of Mexicans living in the U.S. also is reflected in the share of adults in Mexico who report having family or friends living in the U.S. with whom they keep in touch. In 2007, 42% of Mexican adults said they kept in contact with acquaintances living in the U.S., while today, 35% say so, according to newly released results from the Pew Research Center's 2015 survey in Mexico.[1]

The views Mexicans have of life north of the border are changing too. While almost half (48%) of adults in Mexico believe life is better in the U.S., a growing share says it is neither better nor worse than life in Mexico. Today, a third (33%) of adults in Mexico say those who move to the U.S. lead a life that is equivalent to that in Mexico—a share 10 percentage points higher than in 2007.

Asked about their willingness to migrate to the U.S., 35% say they would move to the U.S. if they had the opportunity and means to do so, including 20% of adults in Mexico who would do so without authorization. This is unchanged from 2009 when a third of adults in Mexico said they would be willing to migrate to the U.S., and 18% said they would do it without authorization (Pew Research Center, 2009).

Is Mexico Still the Largest Source of New Immigrants to the U.S.?

For decades, Mexico has been the top source of newly arrived immigrants to the U.S., but with a recent decline in the flow of new immigrants to the U.S. from Mexico, and an increase in the number of new immigrant arrivals from China and India, Mexico may no longer be the top source of U.S. immigrants. The U.S. Census Bureau recently reported that China overtook Mexico in 2013 as the leading country for new immigrants (Jensen, 2015). However, under a different measure, Mexico remains the top source of immigrants—at least for now, according to a new Pew Research Center analysis of Census Bureau data.

Estimates of the number of newly arrived immigrants vary depending on the measure used. The Census Bureau's analysis was based on the number of foreign-born people who said they lived outside of the U.S. in response to the American Community Survey question, "Did this person live in this house or apartment one year ago?" Using this measure for 2013, about 147,000 Chinese immigrants came to the U.S., compared with 129,000 Indian immigrants and 125,000 Mexican immigrants. (The difference between the number of Indian and Mexican immigrants is not statistically significant.)

By contrast, Mexico remains the world's top source of newly arrived immigrants to the U.S. under a different American Community Survey question that asks, "When did this person come to live in the U.S.?" Under this measure, 246,000 Mexicans, 195,000 Chinese and 199,000 Indians arrived in the U.S. in 2013 and 2012. (We report two years because the 2013 arrivals represent only about half of the year given the way the data are collected.)

Regardless of the exact number of new immigrants from each country arriving in the U.S. each year, the trends are clear: Over the past decade, immigration from China and India to the U.S. has increased steadily, while immigration from Mexico has declined sharply. This shift in immigration is noteworthy because since 1965 Mexico has sent more immigrants (16.2 million) to the United States than any other country, in what has been the largest wave of immigration in U.S history (Pew Research Center, 2015).

Endnotes

1. These results are based on face-to-face interviews conducted among a representative sample of 1,000 randomly selected adults from across the country between April 7 to 19, 2015. http://www.pewglobal.org/international-surveymethodology/?country_select=Mexico&year_select=2015

There Is No Need for a Wall When Mexican Immigration Is Slowing

Kali Holloway

Kali Holloway is senior writer and associate editor of media and culture for AlterNet.

If you listen to Donald Trump and his legions of supporters—a task you undertake at your own peril—you will inevitably hear about hordes of invading Mexicans arriving in the United States daily, and the border wall the billionaire presidential candidate has proposed to keep them out. Variously described by Trump as a "gorgeous wall," a "great, great wall," and the "greatest wall that you've ever seen," this magnificent would-be eighth wonder of the modern world has become a cornerstone of the GOP presidential contender's campaign, a majestic concrete testament to America's renewed Trumpian greatness.

Because he has thought of everything, Trump says there will be "a big, fat beautiful door right in the middle of the wall" to let back in the "good ones," which is racist-speak for Mexicans who are "not like the others." If any of this were based in reality and not bigoted delusion, the wall would also include a jaw-droppingly handsome doorstop to keep that breathtakingly dreamy entryway propped open all the time. Because right now, for the first time since the 1940s, more Mexicans are actually leaving the United States than are arriving.

Late last year, the Pew Research Center reported findings indicating that between 2009 and 2014, approximately 870,000 Mexican nationals arrived in the states. During that same time frame, an estimated "1 million Mexicans and their families (including U.S.-born children) left the U.S. for Mexico." The number of departures outpaced arrivals by roughly 130,000, leaving the

"More Mexican Immigrants Are Returning to Mexico Than Coming to the U.S.," by Kali Holloway, AlterNet, May 15, 2016. Reprinted by permission.

U.S. with a negative net flow of immigrants from Mexico arriving on its soil. With that, there's been a resulting drop in the number of undocumented Mexican migrants living in the U.S., with the population decreasing by about one million from 2007 to 2014.

It would be probably be helpful if these facts and figures received a little more coverage at this moment, as our electoral season immigration debate is increasingly fueled by hysteria instead of facts.

Though President Obama has rightfully earned the moniker "deporter in chief," the directional shift in Mexico-to-U.S. immigration is less the result of removals than changing views about this country, a desire to reunify with family and increases in migration by other groups. Pew cites sluggish Great Recession economic recovery, and correlating shrinkage in unskilled labor market, as a demotivating factor for Mexican migration and a possible reason why some migrants have returned home. While the ramping up of immigration laws, "particularly at the U.S.-Mexico border," is a likely contributor to the drop-off in migration numbers, for many Mexicans, dwindling opportunities in America may be making the treacherous northward journey simply not worth the risk.

In the over 60 years Pew has pored over border patrol data, 2014 was the first time "more non-Mexicans than Mexicans were apprehended at U.S. borders...by the Border Patrol." The downturn in Mexican migration attempts since the turn of the century has been fairly huge. In 2000, 1.6 million Mexican nationals trying to enter the country were apprehended at the border. In fiscal year 2014, that figure had plummeted to 229,00. Post-Great Recession America is a place fewer Mexican migrants are willing to undertake the journey to reach.

With decreasing belief in the accessibility of the American Dream, an increasing number of Mexican citizens are less convinced the grass to the north is greener. This is, perhaps, based on more widespread knowledge of the difficult lives migrants encounter, as relayed by nearly four generations of Mexican immigrants. Millions of Mexicans who have come to the U.S. over the past few decades made incredible personal sacrifices to get here, beginning with a dangerous, not infrequently lethal desert journey, followed by attempts to make a life here without cherished friends and loved ones around. Social isolation, alienation and loneliness—and encounters with xenophobia and racism, which have crept up since these surveys were conducted—can take a toll not always or fully remedied by money earned through backbreaking labor.

Maybe that explains why a 2014 Mexican Survey of Demographic Dynamics cited by Pew found 61 percent of migrants said their primary reason for returning home was to reconnect with family. That's a far greater number than the mere 14 percent who reported they'd been deported. For the most part, migrants returning to Mexico from the U.S. are doing so of their own volition. Pew found that while 45 percent of Mexicans adults surveyed said life is better in U.S., one-third believe that "those who move to the U.S. lead a life that is equivalent to that in Mexico"—10 percent more than those who felt that way in 2007.

While the number of immigrants from Mexico has been trending downward, Pew notes that there has been a concurrent rise in unaccompanied children from El Salvador, Guatemala and Honduras arriving at the border. Any thoughtful discussion of the situation would necessarily include a look at the complex contributing geopolitical issues, including the impact of the U.S.'s political interventionism and the country's failed war on drugs in places far beyond our own borders. There's also the matter of immigration patterns changing, as they tend to do over time. Pew notes that "the U.S. Census Bureau recently reported that China overtook Mexico in 2013 as the leading country for new immigrants." There are conflicting reports around this fact, including by Pew's own tally, though the organization definitively states, "[r]egardless of the exact number of new immigrants from each country arriving in the U.S. each year, the trends are clear:

Over the past decade, immigration from China and India to the U.S. has increased steadily, while immigration from Mexico has declined sharply."

Still, the wall along the southern border remains a favored aspect of Trump's policy platform among his adherents. A Pew survey released earlier this year found a staggering "84 percent of Republican and Republican-leaning registered voters who support Trump for the GOP nomination favor building a border wall." Among Republican voters in general, 63 percent back the proposition. Just 13 percent of Democrats think this the wall is a good idea, while 84 percent are opposed to it. That's closer in alignment with the feelings of Americans overall, 62 percent of whom say they are against the wall.

Amidst all the facts that should be emphasized in any sane conversation about Trump's border wall, the standout is that there's no way it will ever be built. The wall that Trump has not yet called "the sexiest thing to happen to border reinforcements" (give it a week) is really a make-up illusion to send his base into a frenzy; a fetish object fantasy for the white, angry, racist, "poorly educated" voters he claims to love so much. Between labor, cost, violations of the law and sheer uselessness, it's obvious that Trump's money pit will never become a reality.

Donald Trump may be a fool, but he's not an idiot, and he knows all this. But he keeps promising a wall that gets bigger and better at every campaign stop. Because he knows his followers don't really care what he actually does, as long as he tells them what they want to hear, thereby justifying all the terrible things they, and plenty of Americans, think.

The Encouraging Side of Practicality

Rebecca Northfield

Rebecca Northfield is an assistant editor at E&T Magazine, *the magazine of the Institution of Engineering and Technology. That organization boasts members in more than 150 countries around the world.*

Republican Donald Trump declared that he would "build a great, great wall on our southern border. And I will have Mexico pay for that wall," back in June 2015, when he announced his candidacy for President of the USA. Since then, many have been puzzled as to how he would actually do it. Earlier this year, in an interview with US television network MSNBC, Trump said that his wall would cost around $8bn, explaining that it was a "very simple calculation.

"What we're doing is we have 2,000 miles, right? 2,000 miles. It's long, but not 13,000 miles like they have in China [The Great Wall of China].

"Of the 2,000, we don't need 2,000, we need 1,000 because we have natural barriers... and I'm taking it price per square foot and a price per square, you know, per mile," he said in his inimitable style.

Trump also said that the wall would most likely be around 35 to 40 feet high [10-12m] and would be a "real wall" that "actually looks good, you know, as good as a wall is going to look."

Putting all potential xenophobia aside (Trump's threats toward the Mexican people and essentially blackmailing the Mexican government to fund the costs of this new border venture), how feasible is this plan to build the wall?

Christopher Wilson is deputy director of the Mexico Institute at the Woodrow Wilson International Center for Scholars, where he leads the Institute's research on regional economic integration

"How to build Trump's 'Wall,'" by Rebecca Northfield, The Institution of Engineering and Technology, October 10, 2016. Reprinted by permission.

and US-Mexico border affairs. He believes that Trump's wall isn't actually that unfeasible, but says "the starting point for any conversation has to be that we already have a 'wall'. There's nearly 700 miles of fence along the US-Mexico border, so the idea that you could build a couple hundred more miles of it is hardly unrealistic."

However, Wilson reckons that the proposed wall is not the most effective use of money: "If you want to improve border security, there are lots of other ways you could spend your dollars and get a much higher return on your investment, especially at this point."

Wilson suggests ports of entry at the existing border, which are the initial crossing points, as the best place for investment. "A large portion of unauthorised migration happens here, so we can simultaneously get improvements in border security and efficiency—which is a big issue—by investing in infrastructure and technology there."

He says there are staff shortages at the ports of entry and crossing points and "this means that lanes aren't open all the time and there are fewer inspections during busy times of day. It also means there are not enough in-depth inspections, which are vital, especially when it comes to drug smuggling."

Wilson believes that fencing and walls are more of a tactical tool, rather than a strategic one. He explains: "What I mean by this is that fencing or walls can drive migration flows from city centres (which can lead to crime and make people feel unsafe) to areas outside of a city where it happens to be more dangerous for the migrants themselves.

"You can be successful at shifting flows by the use of walls, but they have to be in conjunction with border patrols travelling back and forth and monitoring along the border, and the use of technology. It has to be a package of things to be useful.

"You can't expect that simply building a wall across the entire US-Mexico border will stop migration, it's just completely unrealistic and only a partial solution."

Wrong Side of the Wall

In an interview with *The Washington Post* last year, Trump claimed that "building a wall is easy, and it can be done inexpensively.

"It's not even a difficult project if you know what you're doing. And no one knows what they're doing like I do."

Trump added that a wall "would be very effective" in deterring unlawful migration and that seismic and other equipment could spot and prevent underground tunnels. "A wall is better than fencing, and it's much more powerful," he said. "It's more secure. It's taller."

Wilson disagrees, commenting that people will go over, under and through the crossing points. There are already a huge number of tunnels underneath the California and Arizona borders. "You build a 20-foot wall; someone builds a 21-foot ladder. It's just the nature of the challenge," he quips.

There may also be many secondary issues when you're building a wall like the one Trump envisions. There are environmental concerns like flooding, or debris getting caught along the wall, creating a block for water and for wildlife.

"Also, there are land ownership issues. Most of the area is private, active ranch land, where ranchers are out there trying to move their animals on a daily basis. You obviously can't build the wall on the border itself, so you would have to build it on US territory. That means that parts of the US end up on the wrong side of the wall, so you have to install gates," Wilson adds.

"You could be making enemies with the local populations, which are actually your best source of intelligence. Having a good relationship with them, having them call you when they see something, is incredibly important."

There is another argument to let Trump build the wall, so people can feel safer. "If there are border security costs of four or five or six billion dollars, maybe it's worth it, if that's what it takes to have a rational immigration system again and get beyond this demagoguery," Wilson remarks.

Learning from the Past

Back in 2006, the US Department of Homeland Security initiated a programme called SBInet, an integrated system of personnel, infrastructure, technology and rapid response to secure the northern and southern land borders of the United States.

Although it was cancelled in 2011, Wilson likens this programme to the idea of building a virtual wall—something that many of Trump's advisers, including Republican John Fleming, have suggested.

During an interview with US news site The Advocate in September, Fleming stated that "we need some sort of barrier, whether it's a physical one or a virtual one. In some areas that are mountainous, it probably wouldn't be practical to have a physical wall. We could probably have a virtual wall for the entire length.

"Between drones, personnel, detection devices and the ability to respond when people do cross certain barriers, our capabilities are very good. I just want a practical barrier to protect our borders."

Wilson adds that "a virtual wall would essentially mean deploying more of what is already present on the border: more cameras (some with infra-red), land-based radar, air-based radar, ground-sensors along the border that pick up vibrations, drones and aircraft, all that sort of network of technology which is linked to and monitored by command-and-control centres."

Another good investment would be in border communications technology, as border patrol agents sometimes operate in remote, mountainous or difficult terrain. Unfortunately, building technology that consistently works and links agents back to command posts and intelligence centres is difficult.

"There are big lessons we have learned about technology, especially through the SBInet program," Wilson comments.

"Finding technology that is proven to be effective and is already used is much better than trying to make your own technology just for the border. A lot of effective things have come from Israel or US military, which are then adapted to be used along the fencing."

Learning from experience has led to SBinet's successor, the Integrated Fixed Towers (IFT) system, which has radar and day and night cameras along the border, giving a clearer picture to border agents to what is and isn't a false alarm.

John Lawson, US Customs and Border Protection acting section chief said to Popular Mechanics in January: "It's very difficult terrain to deploy technology in, and that's one of the benefits that we're anticipating. This system is going to be a lot more rugged than a lot of the previous things we've deployed." So far, it has been rather effective.

Wilson concludes that "the most likely scenario of what would be built would look much like what's already been built. There were engineering companies hired, security experts involved, it's been tried, there's on-the-ground experience with it and we have essentially figured out what does and doesn't work at this point.

"Dreaming up some completely different type of fencing or wall that is feasible to build and cost-effective in any sort of a way will be very challenging to do."

Dreaming Up the Wall

What if Trump wins the election and wants to build this giant, solid structure? What on earth will it be like? And how much will it cost?

According to Bernstein Research report "Bernstein Materials Blast: who would profit from the Trump Wall?" by Phil Rosenberg, Nick Timpson and Alexandra Schegel, the US Government Accountability Office said the "easiest" parts of the existing fence cost around $2.8-$3.9m per mile. This means Trump's cost estimate of around $10bn is very wrong, indeed—it could actually cost as much as $25bn.

Practically, concrete is the most cost-effective, imposing and strong barrier and would be the best material for the wall according to Rosenberg, Timpson and Schegel.

High temperatures at the US border means that pouring concrete into place there would be ineffective. Precast panels, which are set elsewhere and transported to the site, will probably be used. Steel pillars would support the panels.

They write that "planning and land acquisition would take one to two years with a further two years for construction itself... the impact on demand for materials would occur from 2018 at the earliest."

In the report, the researchers made a base case for the wall as 1,000 miles-long, 40ft (12m) high (plus 7ft (2m) below ground to stop tunnelling) and a thickness of 10 inches (25cm). Additionally, there would be a 5ft (1.5m) wide and 1ft (30cm) deep concrete strip foundation along the entire length.

Therefore, the researchers calculate that the Trump Wall would require 7.1 million m^3 of concrete at over $700m and the volume of concrete would need around 2.4 million tonnes of cement at approximately $240m. This doesn't even factor in labour costs and transportation of the panels.

"As ludicrous as The Trump Wall project sounds (to us at least), it represents a huge opportunity for those companies involved in its construction," Rosenberg, Timpson and Schegel write. "If The Wall does go ahead, it will almost certainly be built from concrete.

"What is less clear at this stage is whether US- or Mexico-based suppliers will benefit. In fact, despite arguments about which government will pay for construction, the large quantities of materials required may necessitate procurement from both sides of the border."

Trump will build his wall if he wins. The question is whether people will break through a physical wall, or a virtual one.

The Historical Horrors of Mass Deportation

Adrian Florido

Adrian Florido covers race, identity, and culture as a reporter for the Code Switch team representing National Public Radio. Florido previously worked in the San Diego media covering immigration, among other issues.

Presidential candidate Donald Trump's proposal to deport all 11 million immigrants living in the country illegally, along with their U.S.-born children, sounds far-fetched. But something similar happened before.

During the 1930s and into the 1940s, up to 2 million Mexicans and Mexican-Americans were deported or expelled from cities and towns across the U.S. and shipped to Mexico. According to some estimates, more than half of these people were U.S. citizens, born in the United States.

It's a largely forgotten chapter in history that Francisco Balderrama, a California State University historian, documented in *Decade of Betrayal: Mexican Repatriation in the 1930s*. He co-wrote that book with the late historian Raymond Rodriguez.

"There was a perception in the United States that Mexicans are Mexicans," Balderrama said. "Whether they were American citizens, or whether they were Mexican nationals, in the American mind—that is, in the mind of government officials, in the mind of industry leaders—they're all Mexicans. So ship them home."

It was the Great Depression, when up to a quarter of Americans were unemployed and many believed that Mexicans were taking scarce jobs. In response, federal, state and local officials launched so-called "repatriation" campaigns. They held raids in workplaces and in public places, rounded up Mexicans and Mexican-

Americans alike, and deported them. The most famous of these was in downtown Los Angeles' Placita Olvera in 1931.

Balderrama says these raids were intended to spread fear throughout Mexican barrios and pressure Mexicans and Mexican-Americans to leave on their own. In many cases, they succeeded.

Where they didn't, government officials often used coercion to get rid of Mexican-Americans who were U.S. citizens. In Los Angeles, it was standard practice for county social workers to tell those receiving public assistance that they would lose it, and that they would be better off in Mexico. Those social workers would then get tickets for families to travel to Mexico. According to Balderrama's research, one-third of LA's Mexican population was expelled between 1929 and 1944 as a result of these practices.

That's what happened to Emilia Castañeda and her family.

Castañeda was born in Los Angeles in 1926 to immigrant parents. Her mother died while she was growing up, and her father struggled to get work during the Depression. When Castañeda was nine, Los Angeles County paid to put the family on a southbound train to Mexico. They lived with relatives, but often had to sleep outdoors for lack of space.

"The oldest of the boys, he used to call me a repatriada," Castañeda remembered in a 1971 interview, using the Spanish word for a repatriate. "And I don't think I felt that I was a repatriada, because I was an American citizen." Castañeda didn't return to the U.S. until she was 17, by which point she had lost much of her English. Her father never returned.

Balderrama says these family separations remain a lasting legacy of the mass deportations of that era. Despite claims by officials at the time that deporting U.S.-born children—along with their immigrant parents—would keep families together, many families were destroyed.

Esteban Torres was a toddler when his father, a Mexican immigrant, was caught up in a workplace roundup at an Arizona copper mine in the mid-1930s. "My mother, like other wives, waited for the husbands to come home from the mine. But he didn't come home," Torres recalled in a recent interview. He now lives east of Los Angeles. "I was 3 years old. My brother was 2 years old. And we never saw my father again."

Torres' mother suspected that his father had been targeted because of his efforts to organize miners. That led Esteban Torres to a lifelong involvement with organized labor. He was eventually elected to the U.S. House of Representatives, and served there from 1983 to 1999.

Today, Torres serves on the board of La Plaza de Cultura y Artes in Los Angeles, a Mexican-American cultural center. In front of it stands a memorial that the state of California dedicated in 2012, apologizing to the hundreds of thousands of U.S. citizens who were illegally deported or expelled during the Depression.

"It was a sorrowful step that this country took," Torres said. "It was a mistake. And for Trump to suggest that we should do it again is ludicrous, stupid and incomprehensible."

Border Walls Are Not a New Solution

Amanda Conroy

Amanda Conroy is a visiting lecturer in sociology at the London School of Economics and Political Science, where she earned a PhD.

Donald Trump's infamous proclamation that he will build a wall along the US-Mexico border has been criticised as a half-baked, financially infeasible and legally dubious product of his bombastic campaigning. But while it's certainly a silly idea, it's far from a new one.

Back in 2005, an unlikely duo, accountant and ex-Marine Jim Gilchrist and former kindergarten teacher Chris Simcox, organised a month-long citizen's border watch along the Arizona-Sonora border near Tombstone, AZ. The "muster" became a national and international media event and gave birth to the Minuteman movement, named after the mythologised armed citizens who were available to fight the British at a minute's notice during the American Revolutionary War.

Describing themselves as a neighbourhood watch on the border, the movement's leaders claimed that over a 30-day period, 1,000 "rugged individuals" successfully guarded a 23-mile stretch of the border from "invasion." After the end of the April 2005 muster and over the next decade, armed citizens—most of them older white men—continued to patrol the border, alerting Border Patrol agents to crossers and potential drug- and people-smugglers.

While the Minutemen were widely criticised by hate watch groups, they also received significant support. They were lauded by members of the Congressional Immigration Reform Caucus. The Minutemen "put immigration on the map big-time," and there are indications that, despite their extremist roots, they have

"Before Trump Proposed His Border Wall, Vigilantes Made it a National Obsession," by Amanda Conroy, The Conversation, May 26, 2016. https://theconversation.com/before-trump-proposed-his-border-wall-vigilantes-made-it-a-national-obsession-58909. Licensed under CC BY-ND 4.0 International.

had a major influence on the mainstream: Gilchrist claims credit for pushing the GOP to start "aggressively addressing the illegal immigration issue."

Their influence is certainly felt widely.

Changing the Culture

The Southern Poverty Law Center, which monitors hate groups in the US, reports that since the Minutemen came on the scene, "Republicans and Tea Partiers have competed with one another to craft ever-harsher nativist laws."

In 2005, Customs and Border Protection Commissioner Robert Bonner announced he was exploring the possibility of mobilising citizens in the service of auxiliary border patrol. In 2008, an essay by Jim Gilchrist was published in the *Georgetown University Law Journal*. Later, in 2011, Glenn Spencer, an activist infamous for monitoring the border near his Arizona ranch with cameras, ground sensors and drones, testified as a expert witness in front of the Arizona Senate Border Security Committee.

The Minutemen's vigilantism may be extreme, but it takes its cue from the more generalised deputisation of public servants, law enforcement and even citizens in enforcing immigration laws. The Minutemen and related groups declared themselves to be "doing the job the government won't do"—and one of those jobs was building a barrier along the US-Mexico border. "We need a FENCE," they declared. "It is time to BUILD IT!"

In reality, barrier-building had begun long before. It was part and parcel of both the militarisation of the border that began in the last decades of the 20th century and the well-established "prevention via deterrence" approach to border security that directed Border Patrol personnel, resources and infrastructure to populated areas, pushing border crossers into more dangerous terrain.

In 1990, a 66-mile fence was erected near San Diego. Similar infrastructure was erected in other high-traffic areas, including El Paso, Texas and Nogales, Arizona. Ranchers began erecting their own fences, sometimes with the help of local citizen militias.

Making It Happen

At the height of the Minutemen's popularity, Simcox began agitating for a security barrier with "separate, 14-foot-high fences on both sides of the border, separated by a roadway to allow the passage of US Border patrol vehicles, with surveillance cameras and motion sensors." Later that year, volunteers began construction on a fence in Arizona, reportedly spending $1m of donated money on a mile long stretch of fence. This was a far-cry from Simcox's original vision but that was okay for volunteers. The fence, like the previous year's musters was "symbolic," said leader Al Garza; it was meant to get people's attention. Perhaps it did.

In 2006, the US went mad for border barriers. President Bush announced Operation Jump Start, which deployed National Guard troops along the border to supplement resources and construct border fencing. In June that year, the Texas Virtual Border Fence was launched; the program put the idea of mobilising citizens to "do the government's job" into use, making live video surveillance feeds from cameras placed along the border available to the public.

In October 2006 the Secure Fence Act was signed into law, authorising and partially funding the construction of 700 miles of physical fencing. The Republican Party's 2012 platform stated that "the double-layered fencing on the border that was enacted by Congress in 2006, but never completed, must finally be built."

Some of the Minutemen are backing Trump, but their dogged pursuit of a border barrier has a far longer history than Trump's campaign, and it will long outlast it. It has spent years percolating in extremist anti-immigration groups that have both borrowed from and subsequently resonated with the mainstream. If Trump fails to get to the White House, that won't put their dream of a border barrier to rest.

CHAPTER 4

Who Would Pay for the Wall?

Overview: Funding a Border Wall

Wayne Cornelius

Wayne Cornelius is professor of political science and U.S.-Mexican relations at the University of California, San Diego. He is an expert on comparative immigration policy and the mass politics of immigration.

President Donald Trump's scheme to build a "big, beautiful, impenetrable" wall on the southwestern border—and force Mexico to pay for it—is wildly unrealistic and won't be effective in keeping undocumented migrants out.

There are good reasons to be so emphatic.

Construction of the wall will inevitably be plagued by a swarm of daunting engineering, environmental and legal obstacles. And even if Trump succeeds somehow in pouring concrete from sea to shining sea, such a physical barrier would not prevent undocumented migrants from entering the United States, as decades of fieldwork-based research have demonstrated.

A formidable obstacle course of pedestrian and vehicle barriers covering about 700 miles of the border has already been built during the last 24 years. Ten surveys conducted by me and my field research team in Mexico and California from 2005 to 2015 found that these existing fortifications prevent fewer than one in 10 would-be unauthorized migrants from gaining entry into the U.S.

Inevitably, people-smugglers would take clients over, around or under Trump's new wall, or guide them through legal ports-of-entry using false documents or concealed in vehicles, charging higher fees for their trouble.

Mexico understandably refuses to fork over a dime for a border wall, yet President Trump has ordered construction to begin while he figures out how to get Mexico to pay.

The administration has proposed several different indirect ways that it says could accomplish that. After considering the wall's likely cost, let's examine each of these financing options in turn.

Price tag for a wall

Independent estimates from MIT researchers and others of initial construction costs run from US$25 billion to $40 billion—a far cry from the $12 billion to $15 billion claimed by Senate majority leader Mitch McConnell—plus $500 million to $750 million per year to keep the barrier repaired.

Most of these estimates, however, also exclude the costs of land acquisition (nearly all of the affected land is in private or state hands), technological upgrades like seismic sensors to detect tunneling, temporary housing for a construction crew of 1,000 workers (if the project is to be completed in Trump's first term) and litigation to resolve suits brought by landowners, environmental groups, Indian tribes and others affected by the project.

If Trump insists on building a a solid wall, rather than fencing of the type currently used along the U.S.-Mexico border, it will cost much more.

But for the moment, let's assume that Congress agrees, as its leaders say they will, and appropriates whatever funds are necessary to put up a wall. And let's also assume Mexico won't pay, as President Enrique Peña Nieto has repeatedly declared. What can be done to keep U.S. taxpayers from footing the bill?

Taxing remittances

Trump has frequently suggested that the U.S. could tax the funds migrants working in the U.S. send to their relatives back home, in the form of money orders or other types of electronic transfers.

Remittances by Mexican migrants, who typically send $150 to $300 per month, reached a record of about $29 billion in 2016. That's been stimulated by fear about possible restrictions on such transfers and the fall in the peso, which has made dollar remittances worth more when converted into pesos. Some of the largest U.S.

companies including major banks, Visa and Western Union are involved in this highly lucrative business.

Trump has offered no details about how this tax would be administered or what the rate would be. It would have to be very high to pay for his border wall—at least 5 percent of the funds transferred. But first, Congress would have to enact a law requiring U.S. financial institutions to verify the immigration status of customers wishing to send them.

Most importantly, taxing remittances isn't feasible because undocumented migrants have other means to send money back home that don't involve disclosing their immigration status (or paying a tax). Mexican workers could turn to informal means to get their money into Mexico-based relatives' hands, such as by using cargadores (mules) to carry funds directly to their home communities, sending gift cards or simply asking a family member who is a U.S. citizen or green card holder to send the money for them. There are 16.6 million people living in mixed-legal-status families in the United States.

Given these readily available options for avoiding a remittance tax, its yield would not come close to paying for Trump's wall.

Border adjustment tax

Trump's latest proposal to finance the wall involves levying a 20 percent "border adjustment tax" (BAT) on all imports from Mexico as part of a broader tax reform plan advocated by Republicans in Congress.

It is not at all clear that Trump has the authority to impose such a tax on Mexican imports. The Trade Act of 1974 permits a president to impose a 15 percent tariff to address balance-of-payments deficits, but only for 150 days. Beyond that, congressional legislation is required.

Moreover, a BAT cannot be imposed on just one of our trading partners, or only on countries with which the United States has a trade deficit, without running afoul of World Trade Organization rules.

Furthermore, were these obstacles somehow overcome, companies that sell products or components imported from Mexico would pass the cost of a BAT on to American consumers. In other words, the BAT becomes a sales tax. How will the average American like that $23,868 made-in-Mexico Ford Focus, up from the current recommended price of $19,890? Or paying about $2 for an avocado, 93 percent of which are imported from Mexico?

Bargaining chip in NAFTA

There has been speculation that Trump is threatening to force Mexico to pay for his wall as a bargaining chip in coming renegotiation of NAFTA.

In other words, if Mexico were to make significant concessions on a new trade deal with the United States (for example, a change in "rules of origin" governing what counts as a finished good produced within the NAFTA area, benefiting U.S. manufacturers and reducing competition with China), Trump might scale back his demand that Mexico pay in full for the wall. Or he might withdraw his proposal to tax remittances. Thus, revamping NAFTA could be another backdoor approach to making Mexico pay.

But this negotiation strategy has no credibility in Mexico. After more than a year of unrelenting threats by Trump to scrap or radically renegotiate the treaty, Mexicans increasingly view NAFTA as already dead, likely to be replaced by a bilateral trade agreement or nothing at all.

It's true that Nieto has an extremely weak hand to play. He began this year with an approval rating of 12 percent—the lowest for any Mexican president since systematic opinion polling began. The Mexican economy is weak—projected to grow less than 2 percent this year—and inflation is rising. But knuckling under to Trump would only further erode what remains of Nieto's public support and make Mexico ungovernable for the remainder of his term, which expires in 2018.

It is delusional to think that Nieto or any other Mexican president could withstand the political firestorm that would be touched off by caving in to Trump's pressure. Mexico now has a highly competitive electoral system. The president's party must stand for reelection every three years for congressional seats and every six years for the presidency. Backing Nieto on such an emotionally charged capitulation would be tantamount to political suicide for the his Institutional Revolutionary Party.

The bottom line

Trump's executive order to begin construction of a new border wall and his continued insistence that Mexico pay for it are political theater, intended for consumption by his U.S. base.

The ways he has suggested he'd make Mexico pay aren't likely to work and, if implemented, could cause serious economic damage on both sides of the border. Nearly five million U.S. jobs depend on trade with Mexico. If Mexico's economy is weakened, either by a trade war or a sharp decline in remittance income, pressures for migration to the U.S. will increase.

One way or another, it is U.S. taxpayers who will pay for Trump's border wall—not Mexicans. And we are unlikely to get our money's worth.

Don't Sweat the Wall, American Taxpayers

Don Gonyea

Don Gonyea is a national political correspondent based in Washington, DC, for National Public Radio. He has covered campaigns, elections, and the overall political climate in the United States.

After "Make America Great Again," it is perhaps the most common refrain of the Donald Trump campaign.

"I will build a wall!"

And, every time, it's followed by an ironclad guarantee from the candidate:

"And I will make Mexico pay for it."

When asked how, Trump has always been short on details. He cites leverage the U.S. has over Mexico, which needs access to the U.S. market. He has also suggested steep tariffs on Mexican-made goods.

But now comes a bit more detail—in a memo just over a page long—first reported by the *Washington Post* and now posted on the official Trump campaign website.

It's still all about leverage.

The memo lays out a three-day plan, using provisions of the Patriot Act, that Trump says will "compel Mexico to pay for the wall."

The basic argument is this: Billions of dollars in cash are transferred by individuals from the U.S. to Mexico every year. To keep that from coming to a halt, Mexico must make a one-time payment to the United States of $5 billion to $10 billion. That amount would cover the cost of building a wall that Trump has estimated would carry a price tag of about $8 billion. (Incidentally, that figure that is widely criticized as being far too low.)

Day 1: The Trump administration would draw up a "proposed rule" stating that no one be allowed to wire money outside the U.S. "unless the alien first provides a document establishing his lawful presence in the United States."

Day 2: Here the memo predicts that "Mexico will immediately protest." It goes on: "They receive approximately $24 billion a year in remittances from Mexican nationals working in the United States." A 2013 Pew Research study, based on World Bank data, put remittances from the U.S. to Mexico at nearly $23 billion, so that's close to the amount Trump's memo cites, but the campaign offers no evidence to support a claim that "The majority of that amount comes from illegal aliens." (Remittances to Mexico were up almost 14 percent in February, NPR's Carrie Kahn reports from Mexico City, per BBVA Research.)

Day 3: Tell Mexico that if it agrees to come up with the cash to pay for the wall, then the "proposed rule" will never go into effect.

Remittances Received in Mexico and Latin America* in Millions, from 2000-2013

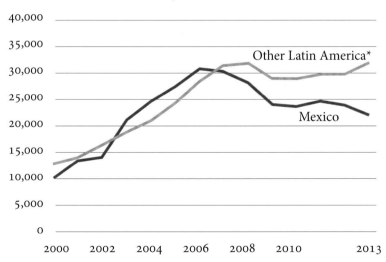

* Argentina, Bolivia, Chile, Colombia, Costa Rica, Dominican Republic, Ecuador, El Salvador, Guatemala, Honduras, Nicaragua, Panama, Paraguay, Peru, Uruguay, and Venezuela

SOURCE: Pew Research Center

Further, Trump says the U.S. can use tariffs and strict enforcement of existing trade rules. The memo maintains that any price increases Americans see as a result of such policies would be "more than offset by the economic and income gains of increased production in the United States." In addition to that, there would be the cancellation of visas for Mexican citizens coming into the U.S., including business and tourist visas.

In short, pay up or risk an all-out trade war with the U.S., writing new punitive measures that Trump says Mexico couldn't bear.

President Obama dismissed Trump's plan as politics and "half-baked." He called his plan to halt remittances "impractical" and said that the U.S. wasn't going to track every Western Union package.

"We've got serious problems here," Obama said from the White House Briefing Room. "We've got big issues around the world."

(Obama also tried to widen the lens not just on Trump but to the rest of the GOP, hitting "concerns" about Ted Cruz's proposals as well.)

Mexico is an ally, which the memo asserts in its conclusion "has taken advantage of us in another way as well: gangs, drug traffickers and cartels have freely exploited our open borders and committed vast numbers of crimes inside the United States. The United States has borne the extraordinary daily cost of this criminal activity."

It closes by saying the U.S. has the moral high ground, and it's time "we use it to Make America Great Again."

So far, there's been no official reaction from the Mexican government to all of this, but in the past there have been strong statements in opposition to Trump's calls for the country to pay for a wall.

Last month, President Enrique Pena Nieto told the *Excelsior* newspaper that there is no scenario under which Mexico would do that. At the time, he also stressed the importance of the long-standing alliance and friendship between the two nations and said Mexico will work with the next U.S. president to continue that.

That followed even stronger language from former Mexican President Vicente Fox in an interview with U.S.-based Univision. Fox responded with a vulgar exclamation when asked about Trump's demand, stressing Mexico will not "pay for that [expletive] wall."

He went on to call Trump a "crazy guy," adding that the billionaire candidate "should pay for it. He's got the money."

That was back in February, and, at the time, Trump responded during a GOP debate on CNN, saying, "The wall just got 10 feet taller, believe me. It just got 10 feet taller."

Trump's Plan Is One Rotten Way to Treat a Friend and Neighbor

Nick Gillespie

Nick Gillespie works as editor-in-chief of two online platforms of Reason, *the libertarian magazine of "Free Minds and Free Markets." He is also the co-author of the book* The Declaration of Independents: How Libertarian Politics Can Fix What's Wrong with America.

One of the great questions of the 2016 election—apart from, where's Adm. Stockdale when you need him?—has involved exactly how GOP frontrunner Donald Trump would get Mexico to pay for a "beautiful wall" on our southern border that would keep Mexicans out of the United States.

Now we know. In a two-page memo sent to *Wash Post* Bobs Woodward and Costa, Trump says he would threaten to disallow remittances to Mexico, start of trade war with Mexico, yank visas and/or raise the cost of same.

Writes the billionaire xenophobe:

> We have the moral high ground here, and all the leverage. It is time we use it to Make America Great Again.

Trump says that if Mexico makes one easy payment of "$5-10 billion" to pay for the wall, our long-term NAFTA trading partner will continue to receive the $24 billion in remittances that get sent south of the border annually. How can we lose? (The Government Accountability Office estimates about $54 billion worth of remittances are sent out of the country every year, with more than half that total going to Mexico.)

There's a lot to take in regarding all of this, and none of it is good or sound or humane.

"Trump: I'll Force Mexico to Pay for Wall by Threatening to Cut Off Remittances," by Nick Gillespie, Reason Foundation, April 5, 2016. Reprinted by permission.

For starters, there's the simple fact that Trump (and his Republican and conservative amigos such as Ted Cruz and *National Review*, who criticize him for being as soft and fluffy on Mexicans as freshly made tortillas) is fighting a phantom menace by his own definitions. Forget for a moment that Mexican immigrants are NOT a drain on America's welfare state (forget, too, why conservatives are suddenly so concerned about *protecting* America's welfare state rather dismantling it). The number of illegal Mexicans in the United States peaked nearly a decade ago, in 2007. Build a wall now and you're only trapping folks here who are moving en masse back to a country that's offering them a better life than the sluggish U.S. economy.

Of course, start a trade war with Mexico and help kill its economy, increase joblessness, and...Mexicans will start heading north again....That sounds about right for government, doesn't it, whether it's directed by conservatives or liberals? Address a problem that is declining, implement policy that reverse that decline, and then declare your stupid, pointless intervention is exactly what was needed!

On a more fundamental level, though, Trump's proposal reveals a mind-set that is hardly limited to Republicans and alt-right conservatives terrified of the *Reconquista*. It's the same consciousness that all protectionists and statists instinctively hold. Everything Trump and the "fair trade" Republicans and Democrats propose is built on the assumption that the government has the right to unilaterally stop people from spending the money they earn and possess; that the feds have a right to tell you where you can and cannot go or even send checks.

As Sen. Jeff Flake (R-Ariz.) told Reason during our trip to Cuba, "It is a very, very disturbing trend that we're seeing in the Republican Party against free trade. It's always been there but usually confined to a few isolated members, the Jeff Sessions of the world and others, but now it seems to be spreading. Obviously, it's being given voice by people like Donald Trump and Ted Cruz, who has come out saying that he would not favor TPP, the Trans-Pacific

Partnership." Indeed, free trade is not simply about goods, but a larger worldview that promotes literal and figurative commerce and peaceful engagement with the world. "When goods don't cross borders, soldiers will," as Frederic Bastiat once put it. Or, same thing, soldiers will need to patrol not just the border but all other aspects of life.

In his memo, Trump openly relies on various "Know Your Customer" Patriot Act provisions governing banking and commerce that were abusive and invasive (and ineffectual) even in their original conception. In doing so, Trump violates not just long-held (if casually disregarded) beliefs about people owning the fruits of their labor, he threatens the greatest anti-poverty engine ever devised: freer and more open trade.

It's precisely the sort of increase in economic freedom, globalizaton, and trans-border activity he seeks to regulate and control that has the main driver in reducing extreme poverty. Trump and those who sign on to plans such as his—including less-obviously coercive trade agreements that seek to protect American manufacturers and markets—won't simply fail to "Make America Great Again." They betray a lack of confidence and stunted as the delicate snowflakes who populate our college campuses and call for safer and safer spaces from actual engagement with anything (even chalkings about Trump!) that disturbs their ultra-fragile egos.

Last September, Reason TV caught up with Trump at an anti-Iran Deal rally. Before he pushed us out of his way, he said this about libertarianism: "I like it, lotta good things." I'm starting to think he wasn't being fully honest.

Trump's Idea for Funding the Wall Is Pure Blackmail

William N. Grigg

William Norman Grigg is an award-winning journalist and author who serves as managing editor at the Libertarian Institute. He has authored five books, including one titled Liberty in Eclipse: The War on Terror and the Rise of the Homeland Security State.

Foreign aid, it has been said, is the process of stealing money from poor people in rich countries, and giving it to rich people in poor countries. Something similar can be said about GOP presidential front-runner Donald Trump's proposal to fund his border wall scheme. Reduced to its essence, Trump's plan is to steal money legally earned by Mexicans living in the United States in order to blackmail the Mexican government into taxing its subjects to fund a public works boondoggle in the United States.

In effect, Trump wants to compel poor Mexicans to provide foreign aid to wealthy, well-connected U.S. corporations.

On countless occasions, Mr. Trump has called for the creation of a 1,000-mile, 80-foot-high, concrete and Rebar fence on the U.S.-Mexican border—and insisted that Mexico would pay for its construction. This proposal has become his signature issue, and mention of it by the candidate during campaign rallies will induce a rapturous response from the audience. When Mexican luminaries—such as former President Vincente Fox—have emphatically stated that their country will not pay for the construction of a border wall, Trump has smugly taunted them by insisting that "The wall just got ten feet higher."

While it plays exceptionally well as political performance art, Trump's proposal suffers from a host of practical difficulties, the most obvious of which is this: How would the government of the

"Trump Wants to Use the Patriot Act to Steal From Mexican Citizens to Build His Wall," by William N. Grigg, April 6, 2016. Reprinted by permission.

United States compel a nominally friendly neighboring country to pay for a border wall? He has often made reference to using Mexico's trade surplus to pay for its construction, which would only make sense if that surplus actually existed in the form of an account or trust fund to which the United States has access—and it doesn't.

After the Washington Post demanded specifics from Trump, his campaign sent a two-page document outlining an approach that should cause misgivings in even some of his most ardent supporters.

Section 326 of the so-called PATRIOT Act, also called the "know your customer" provision, requires financial institutions to obtain identity documents before opening accounts. Trump would use an executive order to expand that provision to apply to Western Union and similar wire-transfer businesses, and redefine "accounts" to include remittances to Mexico.

An estimated $25 billion in remittances are sent to Mexico each year. Trump insists, without providing evidence, that "the majority of that amount comes from illegal aliens." An analysis by the Government Accounting Office in January acknowledged that it is impossible to determine how much of that amount is provided by illegal immigrants, as opposed to those working legally in this country.

In either case, money itself was honestly earned by Mexican employees of private businesses in the United States, and it accounts for a substantial portion of Mexico's GDP: Last year, remittances from overseas eclipsed oil revenues. Tens of millions of Mexican families depend on that money for subsistence.

Within the first days of his presidency, Trump would present Mexico with what can only be described as an extortion demand: Make a "one-time payment" of $5-$10 billion to build the wall (given that reasonable cost estimates are much higher, that amount will probably grow, as well), or the US government will shut down remittances and Mexican citizens will starve.

The Trump Campaign's position paper on this subject refers to remittances as "de facto welfare for poor families in Mexico."

But money earned through private employment is the opposite of welfare. The same cannot be said of the money that would be lavished on the corporate contractors who would be involved in the largest and most pointless government construction program since the Pharaohs conscripted slave labor to build the pyramids. The contractors involved in that boondoggle would be welfare parasites engaged in a Keynesian make-work project orders of magnitude greater than any of the "shovel-ready" stimulus initiatives that were mocked by the same Tea Party constituency now applauding Trump's border wall proposal.

Trump's policy positions are generally riven with internal contradictions and burdened with economic ignorance, and his take on immigration is no exception. To compel Mexico to pay for the border wall, Trump needs to use Mexican immigrant workers in this country as hostages—yet he has also promised to construct a vast new deportation force that would locate and expel all undocumented immigrants from the country.

Ironically, companies owned by the GOP frontrunner have sought at least 1,100 foreign worker visas since 2000. Many of the visas were from Mexico, meaning that this unscrupulous employer would steal from his own employees to construct this asinine wall.

"They have to go—they have to go," Trump has bellowed on numerous occasions. If his border wall scheme is to work, however, they would have to stay—at least to give him blackmail leverage against Mexico. It is exceptionally unlikely that Mexico would comply with Trump's demand, which would mean taxing Mexicans to fund a foreign construction project that, if ever completed, would offer little more than a symbolic gesture of contempt toward the people who funded it.

The entire discussion may be academic. Stuart Anderson, executive director for the National Foundation for American Policy, told the Washington Post that Trump's proposal would expand executive power beyond the text of the statute, and that if implemented it would immediately be tied up in litigation. On the basis of his campaign behavior, Donald Trump as president might consider this to be the optimal outcome: He could claim credit for a significant accomplishment without actually making good on his extravagant promises, while directing resentment at those who impede his designs.

Extortion Won't Finance Trump's Wall

Ross Kaminsky

Ross Kaminsky hosts a self-titled morning talk radio show in Denver and is a senior fellow of the Heartland Institute. He is a trader, investor, and self-proclaimed libertarian.

O n Tuesday, in an unsuccessful last ditch effort to revive his flagging hopes in the Wisconsin primary election, Donald Trump posted to his website a plan to "compel Mexico to pay for the wall."

The heart of the plan is to *threaten* to amend federal regulations so that the Department of the Treasury can demand compliance by money wiring services with the Patriot Act's "know your customer" banking regulations.

Illegal aliens who use these services would not be able to provide documentation that meets the standards required by the regulations and would therefore be unable to remit money to their families in Mexico, an amount estimated by the World Bank at about $24 billion in 2014.

You might think that the plan represents a level of cleverness beyond what we've seen from the Trump camp before. But lest you think that The Donald has suddenly had a fresh new idea, a proposal for "remittance status verification" was actually brought to the U.S. Senate, in slightly different form as S.79, in January 2015 by Senator David Vitter (D-LA).

Vitter's bill strangely would have allowed money transfer companies to proceed with the transfer on behalf of someone who could not verify his legal resident status as long as a 7 percent fine was charged and then passed along to the Consumer Financial Protection Bureau to cover the cost of "enforcement" (though it's not clear what was actually being enforced since the transfer

"Extortion Won't Finance Trump's Wall," by Ross Kaminsky, The American Spectator, April 7, 2016. https://spectator.org/65990_extortion-wont-finance-trumps-wall/. Reprinted by permission.

would still be completed). Collected fines in excess of those costs would go to fund border security. The GAO had many questions about the practicality of this plan.

Trump's proposed regulation would be stricter, banning transfers by those who cannot prove legal residency. However, Trump's plan is not actually to *implement* the regulation but instead to "promulgate a 'proposed rule'" and then to extort $5 billion to $10 billion from Mexico as a "one-time payment," following which Trump would call off the regulators and business would be allowed to continue as usual with money flowing across our southern border.

It's as if Trump gave Vitter's bill to Dino and Luigi Vercotti and asked how they'd handle it. (Kudos to anyone who gets the reference.)

But even if you liked the theory and even if the extortion plan could be brought to Mexico's government along the procedural path that Trump suggests, it cannot possibly work. (And neither could Rush Limbaugh's suggestion, much closer to Vitter's original plan, to heavily tax remittances in order to, in effect, make Mexico pay for the wall. Limbaugh also referenced prior Treasury moves to restrict—for anti-terrorism purposes—remittances to Somalia, a model roughly the same as Trump's quixotic proposal.)

The Trump plan's inevitable failure is not just because when former President of Mexico Vicente Fox said (more than once) that his country is "not going to pay for that f**king wall," he meant it. It's not just because Mexico would never allow such a precedent, would never trust Trump or a future president (of the United States or any other country) not to demand another "one-time" payment in the future, and would be smarter politically, if there were a multi-billion-dollar cost to be incurred simply to buy votes directly at home with welfare-like payments to its own people.

No, the impossibility of success of Trump's blueprint is because the threat of the regulation is made utterly toothless by advances in technology.

Someone cleverer than I will come up with a multitude of other ways that both the Internet and new modes of finance will trump Donald's best (or worst?) intentions, but here are just two:

Walmart is ubiquitous in Mexico. A Mexican in the United States could easily buy a reloadable pre-paid Walmart MoneyCard and send it to his family, adding funds anonymously (or through a legal resident or citizen friend) and at will. Sure, there's a 3% fee to use the card overseas, but that's a small price to pay when the alternative is not being able to help (or be helped by) your family.

Pre-paid debit cards are one good way around The Don(ald), but the platform that may eventually dominate the market for this type of transaction—even in the absence of Trump's mafia-like scheme—is Bitcoin. Two people can be standing next to each other or thousands of miles apart; they can be best friends or complete strangers; they can need to transfer $10 or $10,000 (or much more). Using Bitcoin they can do so instantaneously and anonymously (or at least pseudonymously), with a near-zero chance of being subject to regulation or taxation, although the service providers for illegal aliens in the United States would charge a modest fee—no doubt slightly less than Doug and Dinsdale Pirhana would extract.

If a Trump-style regulation were to come into effect, a cottage industry of Bitcoin remittance providers would pop up overnight. Costs of and barriers to entry are low, and overhead is near zero… what's not to like? In one of his first attempts to put meat on the fragile bones of his many populist policy positions, Donald Trump has offered an unoriginal idea that, for many reasons, simply cannot work. Even if it could, however, would Americans accept a plan that turns the United States of America into a protection racket and our president into "the Dapper Don"?

(As a side note, one of the most incredible conclusions of a GAO analysis of the potential effect of Vitter's S.79 status verification bill is that the Commerce Department's Bureau of Economic Analysis estimated remittances using methods that are "not consistent with government-wide policies and guidance on statistical practices or with BEA's own best practices and thus produce unreliable estimates." As if that's not enough, when the BEA changed its model based on GAO criticism and the new model produced results substantially different from their results with the faulty model, the BEA then "calibrated" the new model so that its results matched the output of the prior model. As Mark Twain (or maybe Benjamin Disraeli) put it, there are three kinds of lies: lies, damned lies, and statistics. The BEA seems to produce all three.)

Organizations to Contact

The editors have compiled the following list of organizations concerned with the issues debated in this book. The descriptions are derived from materials provided by the organizations. All have publications or information available for interested readers. The list was compiled on the date of publication of the present volume; the information provided here may change. Be aware that many organizations take several weeks or longer to respond to inquiries, so allow as much time as possible.

American Civil Liberties Union (ACLU)
125 Broad Street, 18th Floor
New York, NY 10004
(212) 549-2500
email: infoaclu@aclu.org
website: http://www.aclu.org

The American Civil Liberties Union (ACLU) is a national organization whose primary function is to defend the civil rights of all Americans as guaranteed by the US Constitution. The ACLU works through legal means, legislatures, and individual communities to defend First Amendment rights, as well as those to equal protection under the law, right to due process, and the right to privacy. It publishes the semiannual newsletter *Civil Liberties Alert,* as well as many other briefings and reports.

Cato Institute
1000 Massachusetts Avenue NW
Washington, DC 20001-5403
(202) 842-0200 • fax: (202) 842-3490
website: http://www.cato.org

The Cato Institute serves to research public policy in promoting the principles of individual liberty, limited government, free markets, and peace. It seeks to provide clear, thoughtful, and independent study and views in regard to critical public policy issues. The Cato Institute publishes two quarterly journals—*Regulation* and *Cato Journal*—as well as the bimonthly *Cato Policy Report*.

United States Citizenship and Immigration Services (USCIS)

1240 E. 9th Street, Room 1259
Cleveland, OH 44199
(800) 375-5283 • fax: (703) 778-7483
website: https://www.uscis.gov

United States Citizenship and Immigration Services serves as the primary administrator of immigration and naturalization functions and establishes immigration services policies and priorities that are recognized throughout the country. The organization works to ensure proper and prompt legal resolutions of immigration issues.

US Immigration and Customs Enforcement (ICE)

303 Porter Street
Detroit, MI 48216
(313) 963-4408
website: https://www.ice.gov

US Immigration and Customs Enforcement enforces federal laws governing border control, customs, trade, and immigration to encourage homeland security and public safety. The founding of the organization was the result of the merging of investigative and interior enforcement elements of the US Customs Service and the Immigration and Naturalization Service. It boasts more than 20,000 employees in more than four hundred offices throughout the United States and in forty-six foreign countries.

Bibliography

Books

Edward S. Casey and Mary Watkins, *Up Against the Wall: Re-Imagining the U.S.-Mexico Border.* Austin, TX: University of Texas Press, 2014.

Aviva Chomsky, *Undocumented: How Immigration Became Illegal.* Boston, MA: Beacon Press, 2014.

Michael Dear, *Why Walls Won't Work: Repairing the US-Mexico Divide.* New York, NY: Oxford University Press, 2015.

Marcello Di Cintio, *Walls: Travels Along the Barricades.* Berkeley, CA: Soft Skull Press, 2013.

Scott Dikkers, *Trump's America: Buy This Book and Mexico Will Pay for It.* New York, NY: Gallery Books, 2017.

Joanna Dreby, *Everyday Illegal: When Policies Undermine Immigrant Families.* Oakland, CA: University of California Press, 2015.

Paul Ganster, *The U.S.-Mexican Border Today: Conflict and Cooperation in Historical Perspective.* Lanham, MD: Rowman & Littlefield Publishers, 2015.

Roberto J. Gonzales, *Lives in Limbo: Undocumented and Coming of Age in America.* Oakland, CA: University of California Press, 2015.

Timothy J. Henderson, *Beyond Borders: A History of Mexican Migration to the United States.* Hoboken, NJ: Wiley-Blackwell, 2011.

Kevin R. Johnson and Bernard Trujillo, *Immigration Law and the U.S.-Mexico Border.* Tucson, AZ: University of Arizona Press, 2011.

Reece Jones, *Border Walls: Security and the War on Terror in the United States, India, and Israel.* London, UK: Zed Books, 2012.

Sylvia Longmire, *Border Insecurity: Why Big Money, Fences, and Drones Aren't Making Us Safer.* New York, NY: St. Martin's Press, 2014.

Robert Lee Maril, *The Fence: National Security, Public Safety, and Illegal Immigration Along the U.S.-Mexico Border.* Lubbock, TX: Texas Tech University Press, 2012.

David Matheny, *Border Wall: One Nation, Divisible.* North Charleston, SC: CreateSpace Independent Publishing Platform, 2016.

Cecilia MenjAvar, Leisy J. Abrego, and Leah Schmalzbauer, *Immigrant Families*. Boston, MA: Polity Books, 2016.

Todd Miller, *Border Patrol Nation: Dispatches from the Frontlines of Homeland Security*. San Francisco, CA: City Lights Publishers, 2014.

Joseph Nevins, *Dying to Live: A Story of U.S. Immigration in an Age of Global Apartheid*. San Francisco, CA: City Lights Publishers, 2014.

Joseph Nevins, *Operation Gatekeeper and Beyond: The War on "Illegals" and the Remaking of the U.S.-Mexican Boundary*. London, UK: Routledge, 2010.

Rogelio Saenz, *Latinos in the United States: Diversity and Change*. Boston, MA: Polity Books, 2015.

Michael Savage, *Trump's War: His Battle for America*. New York, NY: Center Street Books, 2017.

Krista Schyler, *Continental Divide: Wildlife, People, and the Border Wall*. College Station, TX: Texas A&M University Press, 2012.

Andrew Shaffer, *The Day of the Donald: Trump Trumps America*. New York, NY: Crooked Lane Books, 2016.

Rachel St. John, *Line in the Sand: A History of the Western U.S.-Mexico Border*. Princeton, NJ: Princeton University Press, 2012.

U.S. Army Command and General Staff College, *Building the Wall: The Efficacy of a U.S.-Mexico Border Fence*. North Charleston, SC: CreateSpace Independent Publishing Platform, 2014.

Elisabeth Vallet, *Borders, Fences, and Walls: State of Insecurity?* London, UK: Routledge, 2016.

Lance Wallnau, *God's Chaos Candidate: Donald J. Trump and the American Unraveling*. Arlington, TX: Killer Sheep Media, 2016.

Hirokazu Yoshikawa, *Immigrants Raising Citizens: Undocumented Parents and Their Children*. New York, NY: Russell Sage Foundation, 2012.

Periodicals and Internet Sources

Walter Ewing, "How a border wall would hurt the U.S. economy," Immigration Impact, March 17, 2016. http://immigrationimpact .com/2016/03/17/economic-cost-of-border-wall.

Daniel Horowitz, "The case for the border fence," *Conservative Review*, August 25, 2015. https://www.conservativereview.com /commentary/2015/08/border-fences-work.

Tara John, "This is why border fences don't work," Time.com, October 22, 2015. http://time.com/4080637/this-is-why-border -fences-dont-work.

Juliette Kayyem, "Trump's bogus border wall," CNN, January 26, 2017. http://www.cnn.com/2017/01/25/opinions/trumps-bogus -border-wall-kayyem.

Fernanda Leite, "Building a wall won't be easy," *USNews*, March 9, 2017. https://www.usnews.com/opinion/op-ed /articles/2017-03-09/building-president-donald-trumps-mexico -border-wall-wont-be-easy.

T. Christian Miller, "Trump's 'buy American' pledge may be at risk with his border wall," Salon.com, March 31, 2017. http://www .salon.com/2017/03/31/trumps-buy-american-pledge-may-be-at -risk-with-his-border-wall_partner.

Eduardo Porter, "President Trump wants a wall? Mexico is it," *New York Times*, February 21, 2017. https://www.nytimes .com/2017/02/21/business/economy/mexico-immigration -border-wall.html.

Thomas More Smith, "Trump's wall and the cost-benefit analysis of immigration," *Huffington Post*, October 19, 2016. http://www .huffingtonpost.com/the-conversation-us/trumps-wall-and-the -cost_b_8339144.html.

The Times Editorial Board, "Pretty much the only thing Trump's border wall will block is common sense," *Los Angeles Times*, March 25, 2017. http://www.latimes.com/opinion/editorials/la -ed-trump-immigration-border-wall-mexico-20170325-story .html.

Alex Veiga, "Who'd gain from a Trump border wall? Hint: Not Mexico," *USA Today*, March 28, 2017. http://www.usatoday.com /story/money/2017/03/28/president-trump-mexico-border-wall -construction-suppliers/99749776.

Index